FLOYD IN THE SOUP

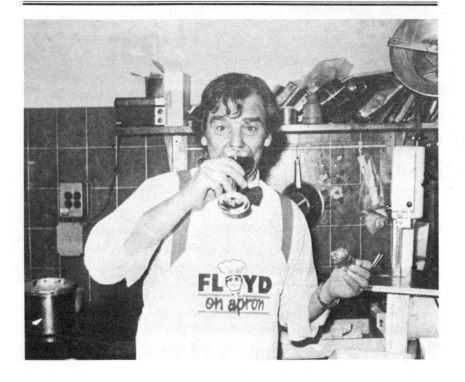

KEITH FLOYD

FLOYD IN THE SOUP

or

MY LIFE AND OTHER GREAT ESCAPES

Pan Original
PAN BOOKS
London, Sydney and Auckland

First published 1988 by Pan Books Ltd,
Cavaye Place, London SW10 9PG
9 8 7 6 5 4 3 2 1
© Keith Floyd 1988
ISBN 0 330 30504 2

Designed by Peter Ward

Photoset by Parker Typesetting Service, Leicester
Printed and bound in Great Britain by
Hazell Watson & Viney Ltd
Member of BPCC plc
Aylesbury, Bucks

ACKNOWLEDGEMENTS

The author and publishers wish to thank BBC
Enterprises for permission to reproduce the photos used
on pages i, 52, 85 and three photos in the colour inset by
Michel Thersiquel; and The Consumer Association for
permission to reproduce the extract from the *Good Food
Guide* used on pages 24–5 © The Consumer Association
1972.
The author and publishers would like to thank the
photographers who took the album pictures, some of
whom are lost in the mists of time.

Writing is turning your worst moments into money

J. P. DONLEAVY

To Zoë

CONTENTS

PART ONE

CHAPTER 1

A BAD MOON RISING

Although he is no Stranger to being in the Soup, Floyd's life is further complicated by Visits from the Bailiffs and A Man From The BBC.

IT HAD BEEN A BAD NIGHT SO FAR AND IT WAS ONLY TEN o'clock. Not as bad, though, as the night twenty years before when I first thought I could cook, and turned Mark Benson's perfectly successful sandwich-bar, 'Apple and Charlotte', into a restaurant. It was a crazy idea now that I look back, but at the time it seemed reasonable to maximize the potential of the place by opening it in the evenings, after the sandwich-bar had closed, as a bistro. As I remember it, Mark's wife, Joy, burst into tears, the kitchen flooded with wine, the sink overflowed and I heard more than one person say they'd never seen moussaka like *that* before and leave without paying.

Nor was it as bad as the night some yobs thought the waitress was taking the piss when she told them the Stroganoff was off. I think they misheard her, but that didn't stop them beating the living daylights out of me, fracturing my jaw in five places so that I sucked baby food through wired teeth and a straw for six weeks. Nor was it as bad as my gala Glorious Twelfth evening, when the grouse didn't arrive till seven-thirty and the waiter, Pierre, got pissed and called the dinner-jacketed guests 'English peasants', and said what they knew about food could be written on the back of a one franc *timbre*. Nor was it as bad as the night when a party of forty booked the restaurant for a gastronomic celebration and I ran out of Calor gas before a single meal was served.

I gave them free drinks and free smoked salmon and quails' eggs, to name but two dishes of a dazzling array of hors d'œuvres. But they remained bitter and unforgiving throughout the evening. Ashamed, I crept out by the back door and got smashed in the pub.

It had been a bad night

NO, THIS WAS A DIFFERENT KIND OF BAD EVENING. I FELT THE customers were not really enjoying themselves and the staff were lacklustre and forgetful. The fact that the man from Access had called in to cut my card in half just before the evening service began, quickly followed by a bailiff wanting a grand for the rates or the fixtures and fittings instead, had done nothing for my spirits, I must say. I didn't tell him that a wine company had already obtained what's known as walking possession of the fixtures – it would have spoilt his evening. He said he always made me the last call of the day because I cheered him up (with several glasses of whisky), and that I was such a straightforward chap to deal with, unlike some of his other clients. (Clients, I thought, how has he got the nerve to treat me like an equal? He's a scavenging little toad.) And I gave him whisky while I gently told him I couldn't pay. Not that day. But he confided in me the most awful tales of woe that he inflicted unthinkingly – and drank another whisky with ice and water and asked what price I would charge for a Christmas dinner for his office party.

Imagine it — thirty bloody bailiffs scoffing turkey and cranberry sauce in my place at £2.50 per head. I said we didn't have any room left for Christmas and cursed myself for not telling him the truth, which was, I'd have rather cut my throat than feed him and his reptilian colleagues.

Finally he said, *'If you could just manage £250, I could hold them off for you, Mr Floyd.'*

I wrote out a cheque.

'This one will be, er, all right will it?'

'Yes. Indeed. I've overcome that other little problem I had. It'll be fine,' I lied.

'Right you are, sir.'

The restaurant business is a great academy for liars. Little phrases like 'I hope you enjoyed your meal,' or 'See you soon I hope,' trip lightly off the tongue. 'Yes, fine, thank you, business has never been better.' Or, 'I'll definitely clear the overdraft with all the Christmas bookings.'

The bailiffs are like the refuse collectors that you bribe at Christmas in the hope that they will co-operate in the summer months, when speedy and efficient removal of maggot-infested dustbins is essential.

ON THAT EVENING I WAS SWEATING OVER THE PIANO (AS WE call the stove in the business), cooking the food and orchestrating the restaurant, feeling inclined to fire the vegetable cook whose presentation that night was sloppy, when the waitress, a graduate in politics, history and economics, who weight-trained, windsurfed, skied and had a passion for starting a co-operative herb farm to rehabilitate drug abusers but couldn't quite manage to carry a full tray up the stairs to the dining room, said,

'Table six is complaining about the wine.'

'What, the Australian?'

'I couldn't say whether he's Australian or not, but he's a chauvinistic pig. Guys like that should be castrated.'

'What's the matter with his wine?'

'I don't know, ask your wine waiter, she's been chatting him up for hours.'

My name is David Pritchard. I work for the BBC. Whatever that is

'Well, will you please find out? I'm too busy to get involved in rows with him, or between you and Chrissie, so sort it out.'

'And there's a man on table three, you know, the fat one with Doc Marten boots and Ray-Bans who keeps wanting to buy you a drink. You wouldn't like him, he's completely arseholed.'

Chrissie, the wine waitress, streaked into the kitchen as the dishwasher stood silently moping in the little passage between the stoves and the sinks, looking pathetic.

'He says the wine's got sediment in it, and it shouldn't have.'

'What wine did he have?'

'1964 Chateauneuf de something.'

'Yes, of course it should.'

'Can you go and tell him please? He says he won't pay for it, and he keeps asking me out.'

I deglazed the venison pan with *crème de cassis*, added the venison *demi-glacé*, whisked in a knob of butter, strained it back over the roundels of meat and finished the dish with a puff pastry tartlet filled with bilberries and some grilled *glacé* chestnuts.

'Wipe the edge of the plate before you take it,' I said, for the fiftieth time this evening, 'I'm going to the bar.'

I glanced at the Australian's table. He looked happy enough with large brandies, coffee and *petits fours.* I told Chrissie to make an ashtray-

When I was in his restaurant I would see him talking to customers after a fairly gruelling few hours in the kitchen below, and helping himself to their wine and brandy, and gently taking the piss out of them. I would watch this floor show and I thought he was brilliant. He would apologize to people who were wearing Gucci shoes and fox-fur jackets for not having any scampi on the menu. I thought, this is what cookery programmes could do with. They're all so po-faced and prissy, we want someone who is actually a bit of an anarchist in the kitchen.

DAVID PRITCHARD

run and to remove any unnecessary stuff from the tables. By the time they were on coffee I wanted the tables uncluttered. It made the people look better.

The man in the Ray-Bans was dunking pieces of bread into his wife's plate. His own plate was piled high with clam and mussel shells, and the tablecloth was stained red with the sauce from the langoustines he'd demolished and littered with their sucked-out shells. His face was very flushed and he caught my eye:

'Hi, have a glass of wine!'

I drained my Scotch and went over to his table.

'My name is David Pritchard. I work for the BBC. Hey, this is a great meal,' he said, pouring himself, not me, another glass.

He snatched the napkin from his wife's (I only assumed that it was his wife. No introductions had been made) hand and wiped his lips, 'Fancy making a TV programme? Would you be up for that?'

Usually at this time of night some gold-encrusted property developer would suggest that with his business expertise and my cooking skills we could make a future and I'd be really successful – there was nothing odd to me about these incredible brandy-inspired deals. I just said 'yes' and forgot all about them. As did the bloke the second he got back into his Porsche.

'About what?'

'Food?'

'Why not?'

I idly wondered whether the cheque would bounce

He stood up unsteadily and addressed the third member of their table. *'Get the bill, Frances, I'm going now.'* The two women looked at each other. They hadn't finished, but dutifully they made ready to leave. Pritchard wandered over to the bar with me and I gave him a Cognac.

'Great meal,' he said again, *'I'll give you a call, bye.'*

I idly wondered whether the cheque would bounce and returned to the kitchen to clean up and wash down. I loved the kitchen at the end of the evening when the red tiles glistened, smelling slightly of disinfectant, and the stainless steel surfaces were empty. I told the washer-up to go for an Indian take-away. I couldn't be bothered to cook a staff meal tonight.

CHAPTER 2

A DAY IN THE LIFE

With some Important Thoughts on Stocks, Vegetables and Lobsters, some Stunning Observations on Suppliers and Customers; and why you shouldn't have a Cheese Board or employ French Waiters.

MOST MORNINGS I STARTED WORK AT EIGHT. MY PARENTS were already there cleaning, polishing, tending the window boxes and potted plants. Mother arranged the cut flowers and made the *petits fours*, while Dad did the loos, hosed the terrace, attended to blown fuses and serviced the extractors or whatever. Mum usually greeted me with complaints about last night's washer-up. The saucepan bases hadn't been done properly, for example. They finished around eleven, had a glass of sherry and took home the linen napkins to launder, and the tea towels. I'd fiddle about in the kitchen, making a stock or boning out the meat till the woman who prepared the vegetables and salad turned up.

Making stocks is one of the most important basic things to do in a restaurant kitchen. If you are armed with veal jellies, meat glazes, chicken stocks and so on, you are

Why don't they use the brillo?

able, quite easily, to create a dazzling range of sauces. In fact, it's so important that even though this is not a cookery book, I am quickly going to tell you how to make stocks.

BASIC VEAL STOCK

Right, now then. First of all you must make a basic veal stock. This is the foundation of everything else.

To make about 2 litres of stock (which will last you a long time if you freeze it into varying size containers depending on the size of your family) proceed as follows:

2kg (4½lb) of veal bones
2 calves' feet, cut in half
200g (8oz) of chopped carrots
200g (8oz) of chopped mushrooms
100g (4oz) of chopped onions
1 large chopped celery stalk
8 large tomatoes, skinned, pipped and chopped
2 cloves of garlic
large bouquet garni of fresh herbs
400ml (¾ pint) of dry white wine
4 litres (7 pints) of water

First of all brown the veal bones and feet in a hot oven, turning from time to time. Transfer the bones and feet to a big saucepan and then put all the chopped vegetables into the roasting tray that you have cooked the bones on.
  Turn the oven down to a medium heat and lightly cook the vegetables until they are soft, but not brown. Tip the wine into the vegetables and continue cooking until almost all the wine has gone, then scrape all the vegetables from the tray into the saucepan with the bones. Cover with the water and bring the mixture to the boil. As soon as it has boiled, turn the heat down and allow the mixture to simmer. Every now and again, skim off any scum and grease that appear on the surface. Do this two or three times in the first half-hour of cooking. Next add the tomatoes and bouquet garni and continue to cook for at least three hours on a low heat so that it is just bubbling. Then strain the stock through a very fine

mesh into a bowl and allow to cool completely. You can now pour it into freezer-proof tubs ready for future use.

However, it would be a good idea to take half of the stock that you've made, put it back into a pan and reduce it by three-quarters; then when it cools it will set to a jelly, and you can pop this into a little freezer tub and freeze it. You will find that this rich jelly – which is called a meat glaze – is a wonderful thing to help you make sauces for, say, a steak, whereas the lighter veal stock provides you with a wonderful liquid for making a casserole.

I hope all this is clear. Now, supposing you want to elaborate the veal stock to make some game stock for braising or stewing some pigeons, or you want some game glaze to perfect the venison in the *crème de cassis* I mention on page 6, what you need to do is to keep a supply of left-over carcasses of chickens, pigeons, hares, rabbits, etc. – in other words, all the left-overs from any of these things. For example, if you made a jugged hare pop it into a bag, freeze it and label it. Or if it was a roast chicken chop it up, bag it, freeze it and label it.

So now all you have to do is take out a few of those game left-overs you have frozen in the deep freeze. Defrost them, chop them into small pieces and brown them in hot oil in a saucepan. Then add a chopped carrot and chopped onion, and cook them along with the bits of meat until soft, but not brown. Pour in one pint of good red wine, chuck in a couple of crushed juniper berries, a bouquet garni, one pint of veal stock (not the glaze) and two pints of water, and simmer the whole thing for a couple of hours at least, skimming off any scum and straining it through a fine mesh. Reserve half of it as game stock, reduce the other half to two-thirds, so you have a game glaze and, hey presto, you're in business – frozen and ready to go.

If you wanted to make a chicken-flavoured stock or a duck-flavoured stock and, of course, subsequently a duck or chicken glaze, you do more or less exactly the same thing, and depending on whether you want a white sauce or a brown sauce, you use red or white wine. Simple isn't it?

And believe you me, if you take the trouble one day, perhaps twice a year, to prepare all these stocks and freeze them (and by the way they will last a long time in the fridge), you will be able on the nights that you cook your wonderful meals for your friends to do so in a very relaxed and laid-back manner.

HAVING MADE THE STOCK, I'D STUFF LAST NIGHT'S BILLS INTO
an envelope, check the wine cellar and bar stock and phone through some
orders. A good morning was when no one phoned me asking for money; a
bad morning was when they called round for it. Then I'd go what I call
'local shopping' – usually at Waitrose – to get supplies of imported French
stuff, like *morilles*, *cèpes* and *foie gras*. Fresh fish and game came from
Vin Sullivan in Abergavenny. I often owed him thousands and, unlike
virtually every other supplier, never once did he give me a hard time.
Except, of course, his van from across the Severn Bridge was often
delayed, and more than once my evening would start in terror and
uncertainty – never really sure if it would arrive at all, or if the order
would be fulfilled.

     Now and again some enthusiastic rep would call from some new
company with some new and utterly reliable delivery service of first-class
produce. Maize-fed chicken, or pigeons from the Pays Basque, or *magret
de canard* that never varied in size and weight. They seldom lasted long.
Lack of real knowledge and cash-flow problems mixed with a large dash
of greed for profit usually saw to that. They charged like wounded
buffaloes. They were often serious, well-intentioned business men who
thought they'd seen a gap in the market and thought that food could be
marketed and serviced like any other produce (say double glazing or car
accessories). A fatal attitude of course. The real problem was that they
spent more time programming computers for the accounts than at the
early morning markets, feeling, touching and smelling the 'merchandise'.
They no more knew the difference between a teal and a mallard than I did
between the input and output columns on a VAT form. But heaven help
you if you were lucky enough to bounce a cheque on them.

     I did once to Hales' Snails and they tried to have me arrested for
fraud! Richard Hales told me later that there was nothing personal in it
(and now we're the best of friends). But he'd just had enough of restaurants failing to pay their bills. Ho, ho. Especially in Bristol, which was odd
because although Bristol has a vast number of restaurants, very few of
them operated a menu like mine. In fact on the famous occasion when the
grouse arrived so late that I had to phone *every* quality restaurant within a
radius of eighteen miles (check the *Good Food Guide* and you'll see what
I'm getting at) to see if I could borrow some, only Thornbury Castle
admitted to having any and even they were frozen from last year, they said.

I don't wish to be profane, but I wish I could call on the Almighty for help sometimes. I mean after his experience with the loaves and fishes, Jesus would be a good man to have on your side in the kitchen. But if you are going to run a restaurant there is no point in doing it except to the very best of your ability. You must buy the best and the freshest of ingredients and you must do as little as possible to them so that their natural flavours and innate beauty can be enjoyed to the maximum.

I mean if you aren't very good at making exotic sauces, don't try – it would be better to make, for example, a very fresh lobster and grill it and serve it with melted butter and lemon juice, than to destroy the excellence of the dish with an ill-conceived sauce. Perhaps even more importantly it would be better to have a humble bowl of fresh vegetable soup in preference to a luxurious-sounding shellfish soup made from frozen ingredients. The other important thing is you must start cooking each morning from scratch. It is very tempting to try to economize by using things left over from yesterday, but you must start afresh every day.

Suppliers and supplies of the sort of food I wanted were a major headache. Cheese was an enormous problem. I used to bust a gut to offer authentic, unpasteurized farmhouse cheeses, French and English, and I was very proud of it. Only in Albert Roux's restaurant, the Gavroche, have I seen a cheese board in Britain as good as mine. But customers rarely appreciated it, preferring supermarket Brie or Dolcelatte. I reckon the British think that cheese is strictly for picnics and pub lunches. They'd seldom eat it before their dessert and bitterly resent paying for it. It is as if they regard it as a ploy to deprive them of their pudding.

You must start cooking each morning from scratch

MY STAFF COULDN'T HACK IT EITHER. THEY HATED HAVING to remember the names of thirty or forty different varieties and couldn't see the point in trimming the edges of each piece before every service. Couldn't see when a piece of cheese was too small, too mean to put on the board. I'd found the perfect cheese basket in the Ardèche and, on return-ing to Bristol, took the measurements and design to the Bristol Blind Workshops where I asked a blind man if he could see what I meant as I tried to explain the design. He 'saw' better than me and recreated the rectangular basket with centrally hinged lids to perfection. Some wait-resses found it too heavy to carry upstairs, others chopped at the contents and left the knives inside. That angered me. No respect for the product. Cheese was, well, just cheese to them. No better than the customers. Most of the casual staff I employed simply lacked any feeling for cheese. And it was a very expensive little passion of mine – the cheese bill was usually £100 per week to maintain a fine selection in good condition, but I would be very lucky if I sold £50-worth to the customers.

      This was one of the reasons why I decided to engage only profes-sional staff, and preferably French ones at that. That's the answer, I reckoned. Hire people who have been brought up to respect the fine things of life. The trouble was that what Gerard, Patrice, Yves or Bernadette lacked in ignorance they made up for with arrogance. The pendulum had swung out of control.

What Gerard, Patrice, Yves or Bernadette lacked in ignorance
they made up for in arrogance

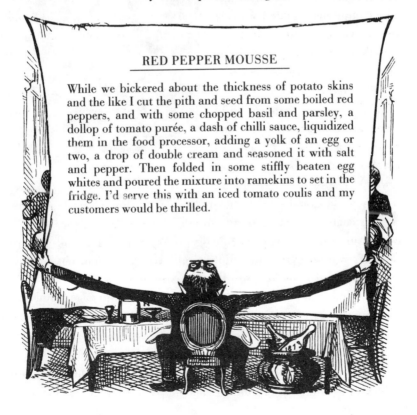

RED PEPPER MOUSSE

While we bickered about the thickness of potato skins and the like I cut the pith and seed from some boiled red peppers, and with some chopped basil and parsley, a dollop of tomato purée, a dash of chilli sauce, liquidized them in the food processor, adding a yolk of an egg or two, a drop of double cream and seasoned it with salt and pepper. Then folded in some stiffly beaten egg whites and poured the mixture into ramekins to set in the fridge. I'd serve this with an iced tomato coulis and my customers would be thrilled.

The kitchen looks good at this time of day, pots are bubbling on the stove, joints of vermilion meat with creamy white fat lie on the wooden butchering block, the sinks filled with fresh vegetables, green, red, white and purple. The tomato coulis smells sweet and of the sun. You've got to get sunshine into food – Van Gogh on a plate. A white plate is a canvas and the food is thick dobs of oil paint that form a sensuous, edible picture. The forms stand up on a plate, a flat lettuce leaf has no sex appeal. It must be placed the right way up like a firm, rounded belly. Make lips, breasts and smiles. Make the plate want to eat the dinner. And the dinner eat the plate. Make your plate sing, 'Come up and see me some time. I'll make you smile.'

Pat, the veg. lady, would look at me strangely. I think she read my thoughts and reckoned I was crazy. But you have to be pretty insane to run a restaurant. Especially one which is physically too small and over-staffed ever to make any money.

Before, with the graduate English roses as waitresses, the customers were happy with their looks, charm and flirtatious manners and I was angry; with French staff my food was respected and I was supported (as a cook), but my customers were displeased by the offhand,

Pat, the veg lady, thinks I'm crazy

but totally professional service they received from my white-shirted and black-waistcoated Pastis-drinking *garçons*. Whereas I was pleased that they could circle the dining room like tigers, dispensing what was due next in a logical sequence that respected the time it took to cook or serve a dish, the blasted customers felt neglected. They, perversely, much preferred the opportunity to continually beck and call my dizzy waitresses, who would have been certain to have forgotten the ice, or salt, or water, or wine. In short, the course was a difficult one to steer. If my customers were happy I wasn't. If I was happy my customers weren't.

After the local shopping I'd go to the bank, have a coffee with my mate Hugh Cuddon at the seconds china shop – I'd buy a few glasses at least – shoot into the pub and back to the kitchen by twelve-thirty, to take the fish terrine from the oven, turn down and skim the stock, and complain about the way the veg lady was peeling things.

Every day I had to tell her to throw away the outside leaves of lettuce. You can only use the hearts of salads, the old flat outside leaves had no place on my plates.

Pat has finished and wants to be paid. She's happy today because there were no *mange tout* to strip. That's another thing that really gets on my nerves, people are so busy serving fashionable vegetables these days – like *mange tout* – but they don't take the fundamental trouble to strip down the piece of string on both sides, or top and tail the tough bits off very thin French beans. I just wish they would concentrate on roasting potatoes, cooking cabbage properly, and cauliflower cheese, rather than half-baked courgettes, unstripped beans and sacrificing fashion for taste and basic culinary skills.

BUT IF MONEY IS YOUR AMBI-tion, get a proper job selling fast food or cash registers. Then you can afford to holiday in Spain, get smashed on cheap gin and eat plate upon plate of red mullet, sardines, octopus, squid, prawns and hake – in fact all the stuff that appears frequently on my menu (only better cooked), not to mention mussels, shark, bass, bream baked in salt, oysters, lobsters, fish soup, pike, trout, salmon, sea trout, shrimps, langoustines and laver bread. They all love talking about that, seeing fish on a menu and eating it abroad – but not here. Really they only want steak, which perversely I sell only on Saturday nights, when the Christian Dior mob with garish furs and pencil dresses are brought by the Porsche-driving medallion mafia. The first person to market designer champagne, Remy and port will make a fortune. If there were Gucci champagne, my Saturday night customers would be over the moon.

Broadly speaking I get two kinds of customers. Those who know a lot about food but can't afford my prices, except for very special occasions, and those who can afford it but should not be allowed to spend it. It's painful when you hear them talk with relish about meals in other places that cost twice as much as mine as they play solemnly with a freshly grilled lobster that was alive and kicking only minutes ago. How four of them could spend £120 in a place where a main course of filthy lasagne is only £3.25 is beyond me. Oh, of course, I've forgotten the champagne (only Dom will do), and 'the Remy'. And, of course, the Italian waiters don't mind being talked at in loud patronizing tones. They add insult charges and feel no pain.

There is a third kind of customer — my friends who love the food, admire my electric approach, don't mind waiting for a table and as a rule don't pay. But they do give a purpose to the place. Oops, I've just remembered the fourth kind of customer. The ones I always owe money to, antique dealers and wine suppliers and the like who kindly eat off their debts. Except they only come on Saturday nights when I would be full anyway. So Saturday loses money like nobody's business.

It's one fifteen and time for lunch. I always go out for lunch. A plate of dim sum at the Mandarin or some fried noodles, usually. Then a siesta till four. From four till six I finalize the *mise en place* and check the dining room, turning knives the right way round. Empty, the dining room is fine, white, uncluttered, with vivid splashes of colour from the fresh flowers.

At five the first waiter comes in to do the ice, butter, cheese and water-bottles, and hopefully take the telephone bookings. Then as soon as the kitchen assistant and my trainee come in I can go to the pub till six forty-five.

I return from the pub to find that they've rearranged the waiting shift and I'm left with my second division — the B team — so I'll have to take the first round of orders and divide my time between the kitchen and the dining room tonight.

DR HISLOP AND HIS WIFE WERE FAVOURITE CUSTOMERS, THEY came every three or four weeks, ate adventurously, drank good wine that complimented the food and always took *eau de vie de framboise* with their coffee. They whispered animatedly to each other during the meal, seldom spoke to me beyond asking about the food. I liked them very much. They understood the soul of the restaurant.

Dinner for Wednesday

Tarte à l'oignon 1.75   Mousse de foie de volaille 1.25

Mousse aux poissons 1.50   Terrine de poisson 2.50.

Sardines grillées 1.75   Asperges sauce
                                    hollandaise 2.50.
Artichaud vinaigrette 1.25
                                Crudités 1.75
Crevettes mediterranées 4.50.
                                Salade niçoise 2.10.
Moules farcies 2.00
                                Terrine de campagne 1.75
Quenelles de saumon 2.50
                                Assiette de fruits de mer 4.75
Ratouille 1.65.

_____ . _____

Gigot de lotte à l'ail 6.75   La bourride 7.50
                                 (2 pers.)
Escalope de saumon 6.75
                              Dorade 6.75
Hommard grillé 13.50

Langoustines à la vauclusienne 7.50.

Rouget à la niçoise 7.50.   Loup de mer au
Sole grillé (pour) 8.50.   gingembre 8.25.

Coquilles St. Jacques sauce rouge 7.50.
Mullet à la moutarde 5.50.

_____ . _____

Gigot d'agneau à la boulanguière 6.50
Pintadeau au pêches 6.75.   ┌──────────────┐
Lapin aux pruneaux 6.00.   │ Cous-Cous   │
Foie de veau sauce soubise 6.25. │ Royale 5.25 │
                                  └──────────────┘

_____ . _____

See blackboard for desserts cheese etc.

    Prices include Service + VAT.   Keith Floyd

Won't you join us for a drink?

'*Won't you join us for a drink?*'
I said 'yes' and sat down.
'*Those scallops tonight were superb. Where did they come from?*'
'Cornwall, but I get them through Sullivan in Abergavenny.'
'*The sauce was exquisite, was it made from red peppers?*'
        '*Tell me,*' said Mrs Hislop, '*How did you learn to cook, did you*
train?'
        Here we go again, I thought. There's no such thing as a free
drink. Somebody has asked me this question at least once a day for the
last fifteen years. I try to compose my face to look pleased at being asked
the question that I dread answering and start off into the old routine.

CHAPTER 3

I'M YOUNGER THAN THAT NOW

A Brief History of the Days when the Living was Easy and Food was Fun; the Rise and Rise of Floyd's Gastronomic Empire; Solace in the Exmoor Snow; an Interlude of Lotus-Eating.

I SUPPOSE I STARTED BECAUSE I THOUGHT IT WAS EASY. I WAS young, arrogant and full of enthusiasm and I felt there must be more to food than *steak diane* in posh restaurants or omelette bars, which, apart from Bernis, was just about all that Bristol had when I started. Truth was there was no competition in the sixties, I just hit it right and before I knew where I was I had three places.

People had plenty of money and were spending it as if there was no tomorrow. In the Bistro particularly you would see the same faces night after night swigging down gallons of cheap red wine and tucking happily into dishes like goulash, moussaka, jugged hare and sweetbreads in black butter. We only had four tables in the Bistro, each one sat between eight and ten people, so there was no formality of booking a table for two, you simply came in and grabbed an empty seat if there was one.

112 Princess Victoria Street·Clifton·Bristol Telephone 37799

There was no formality in the Bistro, you simply came in and grabbed an empty seat if there was one

A jostling mass of young thrusters would stumble over from the pub for supper

I first met Keith in about 1968 in the bar of the Portcullis in Clifton and I can remember him telling me the story of his Army career in the Royal Tank Regiment. Two things stick out in my memory. I remember him saying that the colours of the regimental tie represented 'through mud and blood to the green fields beyond'. This seems to me a reasonable description of his subsequent career, which has always been headlong and meteoric, though not necessarily upward or onward, rather like a Catherine wheel that spins off its post, charges about in the crowd, and finally – at least in Keith's case – finds its true vocation and rockets off into the black in a blaze of red, so to speak.

The other thing I remember is the way he started off his notes on the Army: 'Nobody was there to meet me when I arrived at Catterick.' I recall thinking at the time – why should there be? This is obviously the difference between us.

He has a large ego, but there are many who have worse, because at least he knows it. He wouldn't have been able to survive his multitude of disasters without that.

An anecdote springs to mind, although whether it is apocryphal or really connected with Keith I don't know. It concerns a sergeant major in charge of a squad of officer cadets. In the time-honoured manner of RSMs everywhere this one was engaged in pouring general abuse over his charges. Poking one – whom I always imagined to be Keith – in the chest with his stick and planting his furious beef-red face inches from the cadet's he roars out, 'There's a c..t at the end of this stick!', to which our young hero imperturbably replies, 'Yessir – not this end, sir'.

DAVID MARTIN

Most nights we would probably do seventy covers, except at weekends when I think we hit a record of 136 one Saturday night. When I say *we*, it was really only me and a chef called Neil Ramsey, and to get that volume of food ready we started cooking every morning at 11 a.m. At 6.30 p.m. we went over to the Portcullis across the road for a quick pint and had a chat with Geoff and Barbara, who sometimes nurtured me with Sunday lunches when I was in the soup. At this time of day the Portcullis was filled with a jostling mass of what we used to call young thrusters

(2) Floyd's Bistro 112 Princess Victoria Street, Clifton Bristol 37799	Closed public hols; Sun No bookings D only, 7–1 am Alc 3 courses £1	Rough noisy bistro in the early Floyd manner, with lavish helpings of moussaka, boeuf bourguignonne, sweetbreads and goulash. Moroccan red at £1·25 the litre.

(3) Floyd's Chop House The Mall, Clifton Bristol 24616 Closed Chr Day; Sat L; Mon L; Sun D Meals 12–2, 7–11 Tdh L 50p, D from £1·25 Alc D 2 courses from 75p Service 10% Seats 38 (Parties 18) No dogs	It is hard to get away from Keith Floyd in the tiny world of Clifton's noteworthy restaurants. One member's comments on this new chop house are worthy of Mr Jingle: 'Home-made pâté, good. Whitebait, crispy. Pigeon, excellent. Service, good. Atmosphere, great. Seats, hard. Also had tripe and onions at 50p.' Other wordier visitors for the most part agree, especially about the seats. As in Floyd's Restaurant (q.v.) the main offering here is a five-course dinner, which some find excessive in these surroundings, when they are looking chiefly for an informal supper. The staff do not always draw people's attention to the alternative option, a 'cook's special' with soup or *crudités* for 75p. The original intention to serve English dishes only has been diluted since opening day, and an inspector's hunter's-style game pie was not in fact the most exciting dish he had had from Mr Floyd – but the proprietor is a busy man these days, and standards tend to slip a little wherever he is not. However, Susan Dutch's cooking (of curries, too) is reckoned competent (she used to be at the Black Bull, Reeth), and one visitor says he was served by an ex-Rag queen (not to be confused with a drag queen). Add up the bill: in the 'biblical gloom' they may rob either themselves or you. Litres of ordinaire are £1·25 (30p by the glass, or should it be tumbler?). If you want anything better, go to the Restaurant. There is recorded music sometimes. *App: David Martin, Rodney M. Bond, V.C., R.C.W.B., and others*

(yuppies today), who after eight rounds of spoof and gin and tonics would stumble over to the Bistro for supper. When I left at five to seven, there would usually be a queue of twenty to thirty people outside the door. Cooking behind the little open kitchen and waiting there as the waitress slid back the bolts to let them in was a bit like being a British soldier at Rorke's Drift. As soon as you saw the whites of their eyes you started cooking and you didn't look up again until about one in the morning.

---

(4) Floyd's Restaurant
36 Oakfield Road, Clifton
Bristol 34416

Closed public hols (except
Chr Day)
Must book
D only, 7–11.30

Tdh £1·75–£3

Service 10%
Seats 32
No dogs

Many people who sat under Keith Floyd's *sauteuse* at the Bistro have graduated with him to this chocolate-and-green restaurant in a quiet Victorian terrace, where there is more choice, better food, and out-door eating in summer. His chef Colin Waterton (sometimes assisted by the proprietor) is now doing a five-course dinner with quite a wide choice in three of the courses. The price ranges from £1·75 to £3 according to the main course chosen. One visitor's favourite is the loin of pork with calvados (£2·50). Another mentions Dover sole poached in cider with shellfish sauce, adding that 'the sauce was unprofessional with large lumps of crab' – a more welcome symptom of amateurism than some we can think of. An inspector who knows the place well chose the scallop-and-bacon pie because it was new to him: both it and the apple, lemon and sultana tart that followed were delicious. The first course of these dinners is simply *crudités*: then may come an iced soup, mushrooms à la grecque ('good', says one report) or pâté (less good, and served with poor toast on occasion). In winter there may be hare, pheasant, or oxtail with grapes. Many puddings are now made by a home cook outside the restaurant: this seems to be a success. Mr Floyd says people are expected to occupy their tables for two hours at least, but one member says his party was moved to the (comfortable) bar for coffee. The wines (from Howells of Bristol) include Moroccan red at £1·25 a litre, but after that you pay over £1·50 for most things, and £4·90 for Ch. Rausan-Ségla '61 (c.b.). There is no music now.

App: R.A.R., Patrick Dromgoole, P. V. Roberts, and others

Good Food Guide *entries, 1972*

I CAN'T REMEMBER HOW I MANAGED TO RUN THE OTHER TWO
restaurants as well, but I promise you I was in each on every day and
every night. The Bistro was noisy and patronized by two principal groups
– the young thrusters from the Portcullis, and the well-heeled double-
barrelled students from the university. Add a sprinkling of actors, artists,
sales representatives and free loaders and you had a very happy scene
indeed.

A few hundred yards away, the Chop House, where I served
strictly British food, boiled mutton with caper sauce, toad in the hole,
poached salmon with hollandaise sauce, steak and kidney pie, appealed to
an older and more sedate crowd. It was a dignified little place, but it was
hard to find cooks for it and it took a lot of my attention. It hit a purple
patch when, during a staff crisis, the piano was taken over for a while by
William Enoch Farrington-Hunt – an eighteen-stone sometime lawyer,
tuba player, lecturer in medieval French law, washer-up (I mean *plongeur*
– sorry Enoch) and gourmand.

How a man of his size could be so nimble around the kitchen is
beyond understanding. How this eccentric, autocratic, happy glutton
could actually cook also remains a mystery to me, but cook he could and
cook he did – very well. I met Enoch in the first restaurant I ever ran as a
cook/manager, a place owned by Teddy Cowell and indirectly Acker Bilk
(Bristol has always had a great tradition of jazz, folk, blues music).

One Saturday morning the restaurant was just closing after a
busy lunchtime, made fraught by a little group of wealthy lawyers,
painters and property developers (by painters I mean actual real, famous
artists), who came regularly on Saturdays, spent a lot of money and
usually managed to get a reduction on their bill, because of some trifling

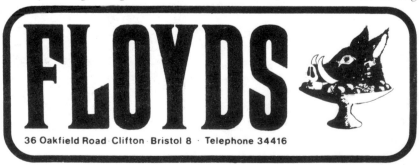

FLOYDS

36 Oakfield Road · Clifton · Bristol 8 · Telephone 34416

complaint like, for example, my old narkovian waiter, Edward Wynne Owen, tipping a plate of spaghetti on to Mr Humphries' white suit (and to the question, 'What are you going to do about that?', blandly replying, 'I am afraid you will have to choose something else, sir, that was the last of the spaghetti') or by them finding caterpillars or worms in their salad. It was months before I discovered that in their humorous little way they thought it very funny to bring in a matchbox containing a few slugs and worms, pop them into the salads and complain like billyho. It virtually drove me to mass homicide. Anyway, it was quarter to three, the debris was being cleared up, I was mopping the kitchen floor and cooking in readiness for the evening when I spied a huge figure in a cape and deer-stalker striding up the central aisle of the restaurant.

'I am sorry, sir', I said, 'The restaurant is closed.' In tones reminiscent of Churchill's 'We will fight them on the beaches' speech, he replied, '*I do not wish to eat. I am here in response to the advertisement in your window inviting applications for the position of a washer-up.*' William Enoch Farrington-Hunt, temporarily resting from the rigours of academia, was duly engaged as Bistro 10's washer-up. So began an intimate and expensive relationship.

However, I digress, not only do I digress but the rigours of dictation are such that, dear reader, if you will excuse me for a moment, I am just going to pour myself another drink.

That's better. Now the flagship of my little gastronomic empire was, of course, the restaurant in Oakfield Road — Floyd's restaurant. I called it that because I wanted to distinguish the type of service and food offered here from the Bistro. Here, in Colin Waterton and his mentor, Albert, a precise Swiss who cooked neatly and efficiently, we had a really good thing going. One of my great joys was to rush off to Port Isaac once a week and go lobster fishing with Cyril and Bill Spry and return to Bristol

Oakfield Road

*Jolly days of Oakfield Road with Gabby, the lady who made the sweeties,
and Albert Satufer, the precise Swiss chef*

with the freshest of fish. I remember the occasion when some snotty
London journalists forming a glossy magazine dined at Oakfield Road.
They were doing a feature on Bristol and that evening I was working as a
waiter and heard them say, *'Huh, look at that, fresh lobster in a place like
Bristol!'* I said nothing, but as I took them the menu, I put a couple of live
lobsters on the table. *'Oh look,'* said the food writer, *'I have never seen a
dark blue lobster before'*, and I said to myself, 'You have never seen a
lobster at all before, madam.'

    Because Oakfield Road was so different and, if you like, so smart
compared to the other two places, people's expectations of it were much
higher, and although in truth the food was very much better than the
other two places and naturally more expensive, we got more complaints
there than really we deserved.

HOW TO COOK A LOBSTER

Since this is a very self-opinionated and personal book I
will give you *my* way – which is the *only* way to cook and
enjoy a lobster. So although you might be squeamish and
not like it, this is, very simply, what you do:

You buy one splendid live lobster, kicking and very
heavy, so it's full of meat inside, and take it back to your
kitchen. Take a long, say twelve or fourteen-inch, very
sharp kitchen knife, and stab it very hard through the
back of the neck. This will kill it. Then plunge the knife
on through laterally, cutting the unfortunate beast in
half. It will still twitch a little bit, but believe me it is
dead. At that point remove the small black sac that you
will find in the head and a strip of black that runs
through the white flesh.

Paint the lobster with a little butter and a squeeze of
lemon juice and put it underneath a very hot grill with
the flesh up until the shell has turned bright red. Then
take it to a beautifully polished mahogany table set with
your best cutlery, crystal, a wonderful bottle of, say,
Chambolle Musigny or Mersault, grind a little fresh pepper over it, pour a little bit more melted butter on and
tuck into it with some fresh bread and butter and a very
crisp green salad from the garden. If you can't face doing
that, then go to a really splendid restaurant and pay
through the nose for it.

If, on the other hand, you want to boil a lobster to eat
cold, which I'm also very fond of, the same rules apply.
Find an absolutely fresh, heavy lobster, fill a pan with
water, bring it to the boil, add a little salt, put the lobster
in, put the lid on and turn the heat off right at that
moment. Leave the lobster to cool in the water, then cut
it in half and eat it with freshly made olive oil mayonnaise and again a wonderful green salad, and a few new
potatoes.

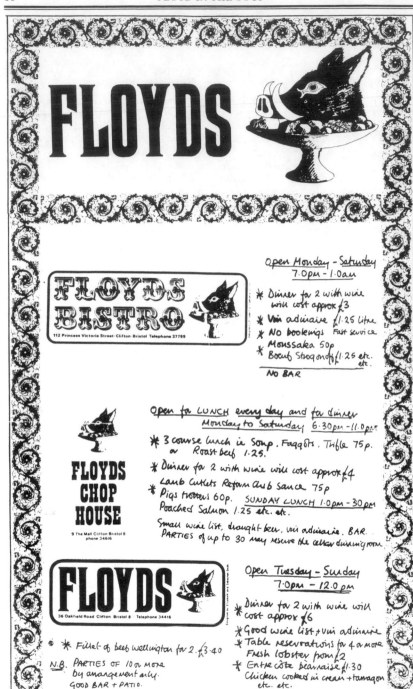

FLOYDS

FLOYDS BISTRO
112 Princess Victoria Street·Clifton·Bristol Telephone 37799

Open Monday - Saturday
7.0pm - 1.0am

* Dinner for 2 with wine
will cost approx £3
* Vin ordinaire £1.25 litre
* No bookings Fast service
* Moussaka 50p
* Boeuf Strogonoff £1.25 etc.
etc.

NO BAR

FLOYDS CHOP HOUSE
9 The Mall Clifton Bristol 8
phone 34616

Open for LUNCH every day and for dinner
Monday to Saturday 6.30pm - 11.0pm

* 3 course lunch ie Soup, Faggots, Trifle 75p.
or Roast beef 1.25.
* Dinner for 2 with wine will cost approx £4
* Lamb Cutlets Reform Club Sauce 75p
* Pigs trotters 60p. SUNDAY LUNCH 1.0pm - 30pm
Poached Salmon 1.25 etc. etc.

Small wine list, draught beer, vin ordinaire. BAR.
PARTIES of up to 30 may reserve the cellar dining room.

FLOYDS
36 Oakfield Road Clifton Bristol 8 · Telephone 34416

Open Tuesday - Sunday
7.0pm - 12.0pm

* Dinner for 2 with wine will
cost approx £6
* Good wine list + vin ordinaire
* Table reservations for 4 or more
Fresh lobster from £2
* Entrecôte béarnaise £1.30
Chicken cooked in cream + tarragon
etc. etc.

* Fillet of beef Wellington for 2. £3.40
N.B. PARTIES OF 10 or more
by arrangement only.
GOOD BAR + PATIO.

I was fed up with one man who came twice a week on his own, drank a Martini as an aperitif, always selected a good half bottle of wine, always ate his food and always complained bitterly about something. For example, his idea of a green salad was just lettuce leaves and when one day a slice of cucumber, a sprig of fresh watercress, *craquante* and peppery, and a little *frisée* that I was proud to offer turned up in his salad, he whinged as usual. So one day, gleefully seeking revenge, I persuaded him to have for his dinner a thinly beaten escalope of veal coated in breadcrumbs, fresh breadcrumbs mark you, fried in butter and served with a mushroom and Marsala sauce, naturally correctly made with veal stock, jelly and all. Except that I confess I did not use veal, I used a sort of papier mâché beer mat which, of course, I had trimmed to look like an escalope of veal, seasoned well and soaked carefully so it no longer looked like cardboard. I cannot hold you in suspense any longer, he ate it happily. And when I presented him with the bill, he said that the topping on the *crème brûlée* was not crunchy enough and absolutely not up to standard. I apologized and then dropped the big one. Bless his heart he saw the funny side and continued eating at the restaurant, and now well into his seventies, we are good friends to this day.

THINGS WERE GOING REALLY WELL, FINANCIALLY AT LEAST, so I celebrated by buying an E-type Jaguar so that when things were not going so well emotionally, to say the least, I would sometimes head off down to Exmoor – past the soft Somerset slopes that are thick with snow like old-fashioned plum puddings, past the slopes where years ago blue with cold and tense with excitement I tramped for hours with a spade, a handful of nets and my Uncle Ken. On a good day by noon a dozen or more paunched rabbits hung stiff from the crossbars of our bikes, leaving freezing drops of blood scattered like rubies in the snow. And I would go on down to seek refuge at the dark Exmoor farmhouse of Ted and Molly Cowell. One winter weekend there was a gastronomic and ego-easing delight, despite the draughts and outside loo, because Molly was a cook who kept a larder filled with chutneys and preserves and, most important of all, bowls of lard, fat and dripping. I recall a meal which started with eel smoked in the huge chimney in the sitting room, washed down with sharp cider. After the eels came a wild rabbit stewed with home-cured bacon, a crispy roast pig's head with succulent meat under the golden crackling, and a pigeon roasted in fat collected from many roasts, with a woodcock and a rook. There was an all-purpose gravy made from simmering a pot of game giblets and pig's trotters. All served with mountains of mashed swede and roasted parsnips – and more cider.

For lunch the next day Molly drew off pints from the stock pot and added pearl barley till it was cooked, then thickened this wonderful soup with some mashed swede left from the night before. Ted had been stalking the fast-running Exmoor stream with a rod and some lively pink worms, returning with a dozen or so brilliant brown and vermilion dwarf trout, plump and full grown to about four inches, which we fried in bacon fat to follow the soup. Virtually everything we ate had been grown or caught with rod and gun – quite legitimately, of course (or so Ted said). I would feel a twinge of guilt for my city ways when he raised a glass to toast the meal, as he always did, with the words, '*The Lord will provide, and the meek can quite easily inherit the earth*'. He made no reference and nor did I to the deer hanging in the stables.

But eventually the pressures got too big, too heavy. Late-night deals with business men who talked of expansion, merging and rationalization drove me from the stove to the sleek offices of smooth-talking accountants from whence finally I ran screaming and took off for the coast, and slipped the mooring lines of my 44-foot Norwegian built yacht. She was common and dirty and looked about thirty, but everybody called her *Flirty*.

I spent the next two years aboard *Flirty*. The restaurant business, like television, is after all only a disposable feast.

SPAIN IS FULL OF CLUELESS PEOPLE – MANY OF THEM BRITS, who think they can run a bar or a restaurant and make a fortune. So to pay harbour dues and keep body and soul together I easily found work as a chef or a consultant.

I remember sitting penniless on the deck of my yacht in the palm-fringed bay of Montril. I was fiercely independent, refusing to dine with loud-mouthed Americans from concrete-hulled boats that looked like miniature galleons who invited me to eat appalling dinners in lousy, smart Spanish resorts. Instead I fished for the dabs and grey mullet that swam under the boughs of my boat and fried them in my last bit of butter and cooked spicy rice with herbs and spices given to me by the Sinhalese cook (or was it the wife of the man who said he had been a district commissioner who lived on the 1917 converted gunboat across the harbour?).

I remember two Canadians who had been given a restaurant by an indulgent father and the money but not the experience or wisdom to run it. It was an interesting experience meeting them. I taught them to cook moussaka, *coq au vin* and paella, showed them how to shop in the market, discouraged them from trying to apply North American cooking to South Mediterranean produce. It was fun doing that, watching the people come in and eating happily.

But life, like fly fishing, is full of snags and sometimes the most well-executed cast will result

Flirty in Alicante

in the hook becoming firmly lodged in your ear. So it was with playing lotus-eating games in Spain. I was living an unreal life – scrubbing my jeans on the dock before the sun rose so that I could wear them crisp and ozone-dried to the yacht club for lunch in order to play backgammon to win my dinner. And despite the gallons of Rioja, despite refusing to charter my yacht to porn queens, disgraced judges and bullion dealers on the run, it was time to move on.

Under Mount Mongo where I lived beneath the orange groves and almond trees, and where the rare, truly local restaurant would fry pieces of free-range chicken in olive oil and fresh, sweet almonds, there was a malevolent atmosphere created by the double-dealing drunks. I knew, but they did not, that we were all living under a volcano.

But after two summers and a winter of this I began to feel rootless and dissatisfied so I returned to England and wrote a novel about my experiences that no one wanted – one of the best refusals quoted the cost of paper as a reason. Next I found myself living in France, exporting wine to England and importing junk and bric-à-brac to France. But the journey every month and hassles with the customs became too much, so what did I do? Open a bloody restaurant again, in France.

'*That was a risky thing to do wasn't it?*'

'No, not really. The French are easy to please and produce is available. And besides they respect cooks. If you're a cook then you must know what you are doing.'

To begin with they came in to laugh, to mock, to see if it was true that English food was really fish with jam, pudding with sauce and meat boiled in water. I, of course, was not cooking English food, just simple French country cooking, but it is important to realize that your average French man or woman is an insular creature, a creature of habit and tradition, and to them French food would imply just the food of their region. And it is quite likely that outside such classics as *choucroute*, *coq au vin* and *bouillabaisse*, they would know little of the cooking of, say, the north or the east of their own country.

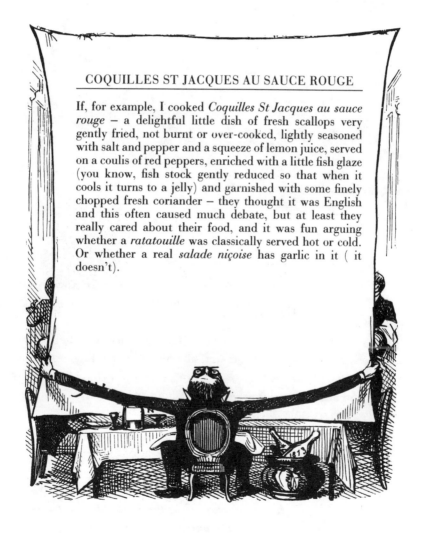

COQUILLES ST JACQUES AU SAUCE ROUGE

If, for example, I cooked *Coquilles St Jacques au sauce rouge* – a delightful little dish of fresh scallops very gently fried, not burnt or over-cooked, lightly seasoned with salt and pepper and a squeeze of lemon juice, served on a coulis of red peppers, enriched with a little fish glaze (you know, fish stock gently reduced so that when it cools it turns to a jelly) and garnished with some finely chopped fresh coriander – they thought it was English and this often caused much debate, but at least they really cared about their food, and it was fun arguing whether a *ratatouille* was classically served hot or cold. Or whether a real *salade niçoise* has garlic in it (it doesn't).

Once you realize that the average Frenchman would no more compliment
a chef than congratulate a plumber or a plasterer on his workmanship,
then after what you consider to be a splendid meal when your customer
merely says, '*pas mal ça*', and as an afterthought as you clear the plate
asks where you obtained the olive oil for the salad dressing, you realize
you have been paid a great compliment indeed.

What did I do? Open a bloody restaurant again!

My restaurant was very simple. I would cook three main courses
each day, depending upon season and shopping, and offer a table of
hors-d'œuvres of perhaps fifteen things from *crudités* to a fish terrine to
pâtés, *champignons à la grecque* to red-pepper mousses and eggs (free-
range of course), hard-boiled and stuffed with tapenade. I took trouble to
get goats' cheeses from small farms and bought what I could from people
who knocked at my door offering tender young leeks, small artichokes or
free-range barbary ducks, whatever.

When cherries were in season you offered cherries. When asparagus
was in season everyone ate asparagus. I am not very good at cooking
desserts, although I do love eating them. If I can just have a selection of
unpasteurized cheeses – like a pyramid of goats' cheese, *un quart de gris
de Lille et une boulette d'Avesnes; un tierce aux odeurs fortes! un gerome
et de petits munsters, un demi-soumaintrain, rigottes de Condrieu, Saint-*

And this is how mad I was – I turned this into a restaurant!

Marcellin, saints-nectaires, Pouligny-Saint-Pierre pyramide complète, Brie de Coulommiers – to finish off my wine, and then bite into a fresh peach with a warm skin, I am a happy man, perhaps followed by some exotic nougat and nut ice-cream with caramel sauce. But to get back to the point, since the *pâtisseries* and ice-cream makers in France are so good you can just go and buy your desserts. Whether it's a humble *tarte aux pommes*, or some elegant configuration of choux pastry balls that resembles a cathedral it doesn't matter, as long as you buy from the best artisan. It saves you time to devote yourself to the things you are really good at.

I had a strange discussion with a French couple one time. You see in Provence a *Coquilles St Jacques* (although I did not know this at the time) is taken to imply a scallop shell filled with any cold fish mashed with mayonnaise – the sort of French answer to a prawn cocktail. So when they asked me what was in the *Coquilles St Jacques* I simply replied, '*Coquilles St Jacques*, you know, those molluscs that come in shells. I have cooked them with chives, a little white wine and a little cream. They are really delicious.'

'Yes, but what is *in* the *Coquilles St Jacques?*' they asked again. Finally in desperation I got a basket of the little bleeders from the fridge, dumped then on the table and said, '*Voila, Coquilles St Jacques*'. Over a friendly glass of wine we chatted about food and the whole business of the French not knowing everything that we think they do became apparent.

It was during these restaurant days that I developed my current aversion to champagne. Contrary to popular opinion, after a good dinner the French do not finish off their meal with coffee and cognacs, often not even coffee, unless it's decaffeinated. They are more likely to order a bottle or three of champagne. And, of course, I felt obliged to accept their generous offers to join them.

Another good thing about running a restaurant in France is that customers will actually ask for a specific dish that they like, but which is not on your menu. So with their participation and the obligatory tradition of shopping to the seasons, cooking never becomes dull or repetitive.

'*So why return to Bristol, giving up all that sun and cheap wine?*'

'Oh, lots of reasons. But I suppose after nearly seven years I was getting homesick and not really being serious enough about life. So I came back and opened this place.'

BOXELAND - CLUB ISLOIS
Section RUGBY
84800 - ISLE-SUR-SORGUE

SAISON 197 - 197

Membre Honoraire

M KEITH
FLOYD

Le Président,   Le Trésorier,

Nº 000284

Just because I was in France it didn't mean I gave up rugby

I didn't tell them I'd returned penniless and miserable and that if some friends, Mike McGowan, Malcolm Thomas, Douglas Bullock, Peter Gardiner, Neil Tosh, Mike Dowdswell and Fred Marshall hadn't each paid £500 in advance for their meals when the restaurant eventually opened, I'd have been on the dole and probably stayed there.

I'd been talking so long that the evening had slipped by and people were beginning to leave. I had to whizz round and say goodnight – say hello even.

'Excuse me.'

'Before you go,' said the Doctor, *'I must say it baffles me why you haven't got a star in the* Michelin.'

'Well, it's up to people like you to write to them and recommend me.'

He looked up at me through his highly polished spectacles, *'Oh, I see. Well I'm too selfish to do that. We wouldn't want our favourite restaurant flooded out.'*

CHAPTER 4

DESOLATION ROW

When our Author, still hell bent on casting out the Money Lenders from the Temple Steps, is beguiled by the Philosophies of Damon Runyan and Chester Himes. Or is he?

THE DINING ROOM WAS HANGING WITH SMOKE AND THE tablecloths were stained with wine. The place looked like a battlefield. But that night we won. The food was good, the service was fine, they enjoyed it; even the till was fat and happy. I said my goodbyes and accepted the plaudits with professional modesty.

'*Super guinea fowl,*' someone said.

'*Yes, but he needs some Cheddar on the cheese board,*' added her partner.

'Yes, I must get some.' I smiled. Peasant, I thought.

It was one o'clock. We'd served twenty-eight people impeccably. I felt great. I felt like going out to play. I mean you can't just switch off and creep into bed and doze till it's time to start work again can you?

Barry Yuilles' place, La Bonne Auberge, was popular in the late seventies and early eighties. He and Mary ran it with glittering style. (Needless to say I didn't think his food was as good as mine.) And many pairs of Gucci-clad feet tripped from white Porsches and purple Rollers through their door to smash back vast quantities of Dom, Remy Martin and vodka and tonics, while Barry pirouetted between tables in a white silk suit, blond (for this week at least) rinse and sun tan, dispensing booze and patter that left your sides aching.

I pushed open the door. Even now the joint was jumping. Barry was talking enthusiastically to a table near the door. '*Yes, yes, I agree. No. Much better than the Dorchester, yes.*'

He saw me and excused himself brightly from the table.

The place looks like a battlefield. But tonight we won

'*Dear boy. What will you take for it? How nice to see you.*' (Then hand over mouth) '*Bunch of prats on table huit.*'

'*What will it be, glass of champagne? Very refreshing you know, or a large whiskette?*'

He spun round clicking his fingers. '*Barman, a splendid whisky for Mr Floyd if you please.*' And *sotte voce,* '*And make it snappy, you halfwit.*'

We sat at a table by the bar. Mary crept up behind me, ran her fingers around my neck and goosed me. '*Guess who?*' she whispered.

'Madame Frankenstein,' I replied. I always did. We embraced and off she went to write out some bills.

Barry's smile faded. '*Been busy, dear boy?*'

'Twenty-eight.'

'*Hey, that's great for you, terrific.*'

There was no side to Barry, he really rated what I tried to do and supported it to the hilt, even though we both knew he had the right idea when it came down to running a successful restaurant in this town.

'You're busy again.'

'*Yeah, we've had a cracker. I can't stand them though. Can you?*'

I hate the work. I'd rather be lounging around a pool in Spain and going to the casino every night, having fun.'

One by one the customers left, noisy and drunk.

'Cheers, Bar.'

'Bye, Mare.'

'See you at the boxing tomorrow, Bar.'

Straight-faced to each one he replied some glib politeness, *'Thank you so much for coming.' 'Look forward to seeing you again soon.'*

They were a popular couple – he outrageously flamboyant and she as serene as an abbess who had relinquished her vows.

***Barry pirouetted between tables dispensing booze and patter that
left your sides aching***

The restaurant empty, he unknotted his tie and shouted to the room, *'Come on you layabouts, get this place cleaned up, I want to go out to play.'* And to me,

'Fancy another whisky? Me and Mary are going down the 'Blues'. Coming?'

'Too tired,' I said. Too pissed off and jealous, I meant. What he called the 'jack and jill' was so full of tenners the drawer wouldn't shut.

WHEN I FELT REALLY LOW I'D GO UPSTAIRS FROM BARRY'S TO the casino and place 25p-chips on zero till it closed at four. I always backed zero in those hopeless dawns, inspired by some desperate line from a Dylan song, 'The colour is black and the number is zero'. The daft thing was I often left with more money than I started with. One night I won so much that I could buy ten elegant table lamps for the dining room. My restaurant was like a demanding mistress, forever wanting baubles and bangles. No sooner was the bar furnished and decorated to its satisfaction than the dining room sulked for attention and needed new mirrors, repainting, a slow spinning ceiling fan, or a dimmer switch.

But this night I didn't go 'upstairs', instead I ducked down the alleyway on the other side and down the steps to Pat Black's – a twilit world inhabited by pale-faced waiters, croupiers, punters, conmen and petty criminals, the odd flushed-faced barrister and an off-duty detective.

Only strangers stumbled in drunk. The regulars would not dare, for though Pat didn't have a licence for a dog, he ran a tight ship. A West Indian taxi-driver was asleep on the sofa and a couple of Chinese waiters were eating toasted sandwiches. The black-jack table was full and four men in dinner jackets huddled in earnest conversation in the dark corner adjacent to the formica bar, where Pat, beaming like a toad behind very dark glasses, dispensed drinks and wisecracks, chuckling happily to himself while his woman fried bacon and eggs.

If you'd been 'upstairs' and lost, there was no charge for break- fast and Pat would lend anyone a tenner for a few drinks and a taxi home. Pat's also served as a kind of late-night shopping centre. Watches and jewellery of all kinds were always on offer at very reasonable prices. No cheques of course. Cash only. As a rule it is better having high friends in low places.

Dawn was breaking when I left. A pale blue dawn, the streets empty except for a milk float clanking up Park Street. Sacks of garbage from the night clubs and restaurants seeped on to the pavements.

CHAPTER 5

'THE MEAT IS ON THE STOVE THE BREAD IS GETTING HOT . . .'

And to his Surprise Floyd is getting the Custom he thinks he Deserves. And more. Until Somebody orders Blue Nun.

FOR THE NEXT FIVE OR SIX WEEKS I DIDN'T GO OUT AFTER work. Or dark, for that matter. The place hit a purple patch and we were packed night after night. The terrace was in full bloom and I spent a tranquil hour each morning dead-heading the flowers and drinking coffee. Even scrubbing the dustbins was strangely therapeutic. The kitchen smelt sweet. Garlic and olive and fresh basil scented the air. And my new fish fridge was packed. It's easy running a busy restaurant: morale is high, you start each day with an empty stove. Chores like trimming asparagus are no longer chores when you know you're going to sell it.

This spell of prosperity will do nothing for the bank balance which creeps steadily deeper into the red because I've just installed the most amazing extraction system in the kitchen. I love turning the switch to full boost: the pan nearly lifts off the stove. Even so the kitchen temperature is running into the nineties on these nights and I have to put on a clean shirt each time I go up to the dining room.

A funny thing about a purple passage is how the customers are transformed from whingeing morons into elegant gastronauts. Knowledgeable and of impeccable taste.

Everybody seems to know each other and there is much cross-

The terrace was in full bloom

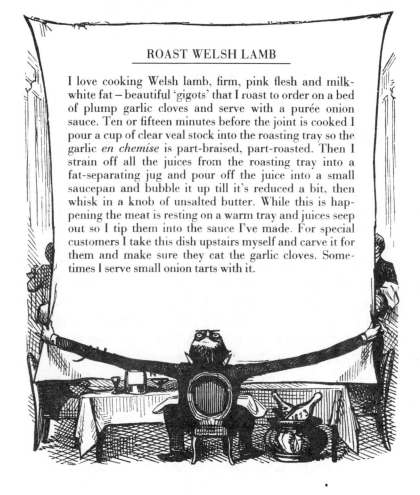

ROAST WELSH LAMB

I love cooking Welsh lamb, firm, pink flesh and milk-white fat – beautiful 'gigots' that I roast to order on a bed of plump garlic cloves and serve with a purée onion sauce. Ten or fifteen minutes before the joint is cooked I pour a cup of clear veal stock into the roasting tray so the garlic *en chemise* is part-braised, part-roasted. Then I strain off all the juices from the roasting tray into a fat-separating jug and pour off the juice into a small saucepan and bubble it up till it's reduced a bit, then whisk in a knob of unsalted butter. While this is happening the meat is resting on a warm tray and juices seep out so I tip them into the sauce I've made. For special customers I take this dish upstairs myself and carve it for them and make sure they eat the garlic cloves. Sometimes I serve small onion tarts with it.

I feel so good I don't want anyone to pay

table chatter. I sit with each table in turn, an Armagnac here, a glass of Château d'Yquem there. I feel so good I don't want anyone to pay.

We should have an Arts Council grant to run the place as a kind of lifestyle centre. There are two tables of doctors tonight – Hislop again and Johnson, another regular. They greet each other with amazement and cries of what are *you* doing here? It turns out they are colleagues on the same research project and each of them has guarded jealously the secret of my restaurant. People are bizarre. Probably neither of them will come again now for fear of bumping into the other. I don't take credit cards – the turnover does not support a further tax of five to six per cent that most of them charge. This has often caused temporary embarrassment to business men who don't carry cash or even a cheque. I always tell them to send the money as soon as they can. In five years I've never been let down.

I LOST MY TEMPER BADLY ON FRIDAY NIGHT WITH A TABLE who called my thin slices of lightly poached salmon with hollandaise sauce and stir fried fresh young samphire, 'dull and disappointing. I could

do better myself'. The trouble started when they tried to eat their artichokes with knives and forks – they were already grumpy because I didn't
have any Blue Nun on the wine list, which they hadn't even looked at
when they shouted to the waiter's back for a bottle. I had the waiters
remove everything from their table, told them there was no charge and
that there was still time to get a table elsewhere. Goodnight. Please leave
immediately Which they did, dragging their gold wristbands and neck-
laces behind them.

Later I realized they'd emptied the ladies' loo of eau-de-Cologne
and other expensive toiletries from Culpepers. Trouble was they were too
bloody ignorant to ask for what they really wanted, which was a crispy
duck or a well-done steak. Funny thing is, I'd have cooked that for them
with pleasure if they'd had the sense to ask. (Yes, I know I said earlier I
only serve steaks on Saturday – but because I hang my own meat in fact I
always have some in stock.)

Things were going well, the weather was fine and I opened for
Sunday lunch. I laid tables on the terrace, fired up the charcoal grill and
whacked out grilled sardines, prawns, *salades niçoises*, paella, couscous
and all manner of Provençal delights. Of course they really wanted roast
beef, but with the support of people like Barry and Cuddon, who sometimes dragged unwilling friends to lunch at their expense, the thing took
off. Some Sundays we'd take more than a Saturday night – mainly
because of the terrific booze consumption.

Then as suddenly as the rush had started six or so weeks before, it
stopped, and we were back to doing between ten and twenty-five people a
night. I wouldn't trim my culinary sails, of course, kept on buying the
same quantities and varieties of food just in case, and the bank account
slid deeper into the red.

FLOYDS BISTRO

112 Princess Victoria Street · Clifton · Bristol Telephone 37799

CHAPTER 6

GUESS WHO ISN'T COMING TO DINNER?

A Time when our Hero discovers that Street Credibility doesn't open any Doors.

SO MANY WELL-KNOWN PEOPLE VISITED THE RESTAURANT I can't remember them all – I should have kept a visitors' book I suppose. Leonard Rossiter was a regular when in Bristol: he usually came with David Martin. He loved the place, and when I published my first cookbook he wrote a foward for it, which was great. I was very sad when he died. Frank Muir, Paul Eddington, Gerald Scarfe, the Monty Python team, one of them spent the whole evening after dinner washing up – said it was a pleasure to do something useful. George Melly, who told the most superb jokes, that great actor who kept playing Winston Churchill and someone in 'All Creatures Great and Small' – I forget his name, but his daughter used to waitress in the place. Then there was the night a waitress refused to work because she said one of the surgeons from her hospital (she was a medical student) was in eating, but in fact he turned out to be an actor from some TV medical series. So she did. And got his autograph. Then there was the night Peter O'Toole didn't turn up. Customers who got wind he was coming hung on in the hope of seeing him (as a rule we never told people who was coming), but were rewarded with Patrick Dromgoole making a superb entrance, pausing at the door and saying,

'Keith love, Peter's so sorry, he's too tired to come, but sends his love.'

But the most exciting non-event was when Mick Jagger and the Rolling Stones didn't come. They were doing a concert in Bristol and a pal of mine works with Harvey Gold-smith — indeed they'd been into the restaurant with two brief-cases, one full of Stones' tickets and one full of money — and Mike Good who knows the Stones, in fact knows everybody in the rock business, said he'd been asked by Mick to book three restaurants, an Indian, a Chinese and mine — just in case they felt like eating. We all got very excited — of course, we were sworn to secrecy and nobody else would be allowed into the place — but, of course, it didn't happen. Though as usual word did get out, and for a while all the other restaurants were very jealous.

My place attracted more than its fair share of media people, too. The BBC or HTV would often book tables of eight, ten or twelve, and a film crew, the director, one of the stars or a presenter and a couple of assis-tants would duly roll up, usually an hour late, always at least six more or *less* than they'd booked for (two of whom would be veg-etarians, of course, and a third would only eat caviar and larks' tongues on toast). Then be in a desperate hurry, then hog the phone one after the other in very loud voices with identical conver-sations, e.g.:

'What about lunch, Pat?' I said. We were making a television film in Bristol, my favourite city, and as we were to be there for more than three weeks catering arrangements were going to be important. Normally a film unit is fed by strange men who follow you around in a small lorry. 'Ah,' said Pat Dromgoole our director, 'we're going to Keith Floyd's in Clifton.' This was in the early 1970s. The first meal was so good that afterwards I remember saying to Pat, 'never mind the filming, let's just make sure Keith can fit us in every day.'

From that time on whenever I have visited Bristol a meal at one of Keith's restaurants is a pleasure to which I have always looked forward. Obviously his food is good or I wouldn't be writing this, but above all there is always that one essential quality, you are made to feel that the meal you are having is Keith's most important job that day. I can think of no higher praise.

LEONARD ROSSITER

'Ya, it's me. No. At Floyd's restaurant. Any messages? Ya. Right. No awful. Can't talk now, tell you later. And if . . . rings, tell him I'm busy with . . .'

Then, worst of all, they all wanted separate, itemized bills, asked sweetly if service was included and left no tip without hearing the reply, stuffed the pockets of their anoraks with fruit, cheese and *petits fours*, took the unfinished wine and left. Promising, God help me, to recommend me to their colleagues.

Of course, all these people are very pleasant to one. In fact, being a cook you get lots of praise and attention and they treat you as a great friend – *in* the restaurant. Outside it's a little different. Like they'd never actually invite you for dinner (contrary to what they say as they stumble out of your door, pissed).

It's important for cooks to remember that we are, well, just cooks. Bit like a plumber really. Or a shop assistant. I mean you wouldn't want that sort of person at your table would you? Should the conversation turn from cooking as it sometimes does and you,

By the way, lots of ordinary people did not turn up either, especially at Christmas time when the great trick is for, say, three or four couples getting together for a big night out each to book their favourite place for eight people, meet in the pub, or at home for a few stiff drinks, then decide which of the four places they've booked to go to. Of course they don't ring to cancel the other three and since they've booked for eight-thirty to nine and since everybody wants to eat at that time, by the time the penny drops that they are not coming you can't re-book the table. And, of course, earlier in the evening you refused chance bookings. I think that failure to cancel a booked table – even with the feeblest of excuses – should be made at least a hanging offence, if not drawing and quartering too.

say, discuss a well-known book or pass comment on some piece of current affairs, you often see a quizzical look on their faces. Or if by chance they bump into you at the theatre they say, *'What on earth are you doing here? I didn't know you liked Shakespeare. You really must come for dinner sometime. I'll get the wife to sort it out.'*

CHAPTER 7

I AM THE MORNING DJ ON W.O.L.D.

But a Series of Altercations with the lovely Rita leaves him just another Fallen Star waiting for the Early Train.

IN THE SUMMER OF 1981 OR '82, I CAN'T REMEMBER WHICH, I published a little cookbook called *Floyd's Food*. It, as most things in my life, happened more or less by accident. A Bath publisher, Jon Croft, was producing a book of West Country restaurant recipes and asked me to contribute to it, which I did. He then produced a second one. Ditto performance. No fee of course. When he came to collect the second contribution I casually mentioned that if he ever wanted me to do a whole book I'd be delighted. So the idea was born and I hurriedly wrote it. It sold two or three thousand copies, mainly in the West Country, and disappeared from view. But it was very exciting and I was (and still am) jolly proud of it. The local papers reviewed it favourably. The local radio stations interviewed me – I felt quite a little star – and I earned about £600, I think. Which went towards the VAT, naturally. Well it should have done, but in fact I bought an icemaker and a Magimix.

The addition of which to the *batterie de cuisine* transformed the preparation of egg-liaison sauce-making from an art to a simple cooking-by-numbers routine. Any implement that saves you time – without compromising the end result – is OK by me. Microwaves included. I don't use a microwave for real cooking – I mean, no matter what the manufacturers say you're mad if you roast your Sunday joint in one – but in many other ways, e.g. reheating vegetables or servings of sauce, they are invaluable.

Floyd's Food was not exactly the definitive cookbook, but many people who bought a copy told me they thought it was great, and that's a

Floyd's FOOD

a cookbook by
Keith Floyd

Foreword by
Leonard Rossiter

good feeling. Anyway, I rolled up to Bristol's new independent radio station, Radio West, to be interviewed by John Hayes on the Morning Show, where I met two legendary DJs of the pirate radio era, Dave Cash and Johnny Walker. They added a lot of style to the shows. Hayes and I got on really fine, we plugged the book like mad and chattered on air for three-quarters of an hour. After the show we chatted to Dave Cash who was the station manager. He asked me to do a food spot on Hayes' show every morning. Yippee. 'You bet,' I said. *'No fee, of course,'* he said.

John Hayes was brilliant. After a couple of mornings of him leading my item through the question-and-answer process till I was at ease with the little studio, he just let me get on with it. To begin with I'd do a simple recipe and explain how to cook it. But little by little, with John's help, I expanded it into restaurant reports, recipes and chatted about last night's activities in the restaurant.

One morning I read a short story by Saki, on another gave a lecture on restaurant manners and named the people who'd behaved appallingly the night before. Anything went – it became a sort of cross between Nigel Dempster and the 'Food and Drink Programme'. If I was late (I had to be at the studio after the nine o'clock bulletin), I'd pretend my chauffeur was late reporting for duty and that sort of thing. It was great fun and we got a good audience. Everybody was pleased. Especially me.

Sometimes we cooked on air, in the station kitchen, with John linking through the studio. Once I dried for a moment – carried away flaming a lobster in cognac – on the wireless for God's sake – and John tried to bring me back with the question, *'What's the weather like where you are, Floyd?'* Without a thought of being live I said it was pissing down. Oops – I never dried again.

Then there was the day the IBA told me off for referring to some (unnamed) person as a bit of a poof. After the show John told me the managing director wanted to see me.

'What for?'

'I don't know,' he said.

I was expecting the sack, but to my delight he offered me my own show – a half-an-hour show once a week at eight o'clock, the 'Floyd Phone In'. *'Of course we can't afford to pay you, you understand.'* I understood.

*'Keith Floyd, restaurateur,
writer, broadcaster'*

I raced up to Clifton, dragged Cuddon out of his shop and celebrated with vodka and orange juices in the Greyhound. (Once one of the great Bristol pubs when Henry and Barbara ran it for the beatniks, painters, writers and layabouts of the fifties and sixties. It's still more or less OK now – if you like financial services brokers and two-year-old Porsches. Be that as it may, I've been drinking there for more than twenty years, so why change now?) I was cock-a-hoop I can tell you. My own radio show, not to mention the publicity for the restaurant.

'How much are they paying you?'

I was thinking how good 'Keith Floyd, restaurateur, writer, broadcaster . . .' sounded.

'Sorry?'

Cuddon said, *'How much are they paying you?'*

'Nothing, but I don't mind, it's good for the restaurant.'

'You will, old scout, you will.'

'Don't be so miserable, let's have another.'

After the news there was the station-identification jingle, 'Making it special with Radio West, we've got a good thing going.'

Then the red light, then my signature tune. I sat at the console with my knees knocking and my throat taut and dry. Scared shitless. It was OK with John Hayes, but now, here and on my own, was quite different. My music was called 'Bits and Pieces', an aggressive little number.

It faded.

'Good evening world, this is Keith Floyd with thirty minutes of fun on the phone. Here on Radio West. So if you've something you'd like to talk about, rant about, laugh about or shout about, call me now on Bristol 279238. The lines are open now.'

So far so good. I'd opened the programme. All I had to do now was keep talking till someone called. What if they didn't? I ringed a few controversial stories in the papers and trawled some ideas to the world listening (?) outside in the night. Praying for the phone lines to light up. I was just launching into the pros and cons of a German court case where a woman had shot the man who raped her daughter, when the first call came through. I was up and running.

Then another call, so I cut my first caller out, suggesting he called when he had less time. In a flash it was over. I was trembling and sweating and in desperate need of a Scotch when I came off air. 'Making it special with Radio West, we've got a good thing going.' I wanted to know how I did, but was too proud to ask. After a few more weeks of this and my daily spot with John Hayes, I decided to ask for money. Yes, they said, no problem. Six pounds per night. Get stuffed, I said, and we parted company.

That was the end of my broadcasting career.

I expect they thought I was star-struck. I felt ripped off. I mean six quid – still no payment for the morning slot, mark you, and that cost me a parking ticket each morning. And on Thursday nights I opened the restaurant later to take in my show. Still, it had been fun. And I did privately regret storming out. I missed the thrill and power of radio, even if it was a two-bit local station. Cuddon said, '*I told you so*'.

The trouble was I had a real taste for the business. I missed it like hell. Shortly afterwards they had a management shake-up and I nearly called them to ask for a job. Again I was too proud. Bloody minded and stubborn even.

CHAPTER 8

MEMPHIS BLUES

A short Disquisition on a subject dear to Floyd's Heart: the British Tourist Industry and why the Prime Minister should make him Minister for Tourism. Followed by another Brief Flirtation with the Media.

I FELT FLAT. THE EXCITEMENT OF THE BOOK HAD LONG faded and now there was no radio programme either. Just the frying pan, and late-night drinking in Pat Black's. It was November. The book, summer and the Sunday lunches on the terrace were long gone.

There were staff problems too – the French waiters had gone, either fired for getting drunk or they just hadn't returned from their holidays. Of course, I'd pay them holiday money and lend them the airfare and all that guff. So I was breaking in a new team of students and

36 OAKFIELD ROAD.

a couple of YOPS in the kitchen. It's incredible. I advertised locally and nationally for kitchen staff – young chefs with some experience and a knowledge of French food, etc. etc. and there were no replies at all except for a couple of dolly girls who'd done a Cordon-Bleu course, at great expense to their parents no doubt.

They were even worse than the run-of-the-mill graduate from a British catering college. Considering that about the only worth-while industry this country's got left is tourism, it's time Mrs Thatcher spent some money on proper training facilities for cooks and waiters.

The average standard of expertise, not to mention willingness to work, is disgraceful. She should appoint a minister (me) and a committee of people like Albert Roux to get a training scheme going. No, the only way to get staff at present is to get them really young, before they've been ruined by cowboy practices, and train them yourself. But it's an uphill task trying to implant a sense of taste and style into a kid that's been brought up on frozen pizza, hamburgers and beans.

Also there should be a serious government classification of restaurants and hotels with strict requirements for licences to operate, as well as a realistic campaign to encourage British cooking. It shouldn't be left to a few visionaries working alone. And catering shouldn't be something kids drift into simply because the plumbing course was over-subscribed.

I NEEDED A LIFT, SOME EXCITEMENT TO TAKE THE PLACE OF
the radio station, and as usual the restaurant provided it. I decided to go
over the top on game. We started serving pheasant and rabbit and hare
and goat and quail and partridge . . . And the punters loved it.

Dinner for Saturday

Consommé de gibier 1·75   Potage St. Germain 1·50
Moules à la marinières 2·75   Tarte à l'oignon 1·75
Oeuf en cocotte 1·50.   Tarte de poisson 2·10
Panaché de champignons sauvage 3·75. Terrine de gibier 1·75
Fromage de chèvre grillé au noix 2·20
Magret de canard fumé 3·20 Croustade de fruits
Les huitres (6) 3·50.   de mer. 3·75

| See blackboard for desserts
| cheese salads etc.

Faisan à la normande   6·75.
Rable du lièvre à la crème 6·50.
Canard du barbarie rôti   7·25.
Civet du lièvre 5·75
Chevreuil à la crème de cassis 8·00
Perdrix rôti 7·25.
Caille rôti à la provençale 6·00.
Perdrix au choux 6·95
Queue de boeuf aux oignons 5·25.
Cassoulet 5·00.
Choucroute 5·00. _
Entrecôte bordelaise 7·50.
Coquilles St. Jacques "St. Hubert" 7·50.
Filet de bar sauce rouge 7·50.
Panaché de poisson et crustaces à la Chinoise 9·10.
      Service + VAT included.   ceilidflons

The restaurant was back on course, but I was getting anxious letters from the bank manager. Surely now after three years we should be seeing a turnaround? he wrote. Perhaps you would arrange to see me in the near future? I'd have to see him, but the problem is I had nothing new to say. I was doing my best, but we were just not getting enough business. The only sure way of increasing turnover is to reduce the prices and offer them what they really want, which is a full stomach and a piss up for about eight to ten pounds a head. I couldn't do it. I called his secretary to see him the following week. And yes, I'd bring the figures. The other insoluble problem was that I started the place desperately under-capitalized. And only an injection of capital – which on present business I couldn't service – would or might have changed things.

Then I got an excited call from a friend at HTV who'd just read my book and was anxious to 'fix something up'. We had lunch and I was surprised how vague he was about my possible involvement in an after-noon magazine programme. I assumed he'd say we want you to do so and so. However, I was to choose six recipes from the book and roll up to the studio with the ingredients and equipment and he would record six to eight minutes' cooking slots to drop in each week. And I'd get six hundred pounds. More than enough to put down a deposit on an espresso coffee machine.

My performance to say the least was forgettable. There were three or four cameras and hundreds of people hanging around, none of whom spoke to me or offered any advice or assistance whatsoever.

I didn't know which camera to look at. After it was all over the press office phoned to comment on the vast number of complaints they'd received about me using my fingers and not spoons, and worst of all what had I to say about roasting a guinea fowl and leaving the plastic bag of giblets inside – apparently revealed for all to see when I cut the bird in half.

I said, why had no one noticed on the day we recorded – there were enough of you watching. Obviously I wouldn't have done it on purpose and surely they could have edited that bit out. The woman's tone was too brusque for my liking and I told her so. And what I thought of her TV station. They didn't call me again. My one big chance had come and gone. I was beginning to get the message. First Radio West, now HTV, clearly the media was not for me. And judging by my meeting with the bank manager, neither was the restaurant business.

Although he was amicable enough and indeed was a valued customer of the place, he gave me six months to get it right or he'd have to call in the loan. I said, 'Look, if you lend me thirty thousand, I can clear the overdraft, pay the VAT, clear all the creditors and start fresh, then I wouldn't be chasing my tail the whole time.' He agreed, I signed over the deeds of the property and stepped out of the bank full of confidence and resolve. It was the worst decision I've ever made in my life. I cleared up the creditors at once, overspent on equipment and improvements, hired permanent staff, had menus printed – the whole nine yards.

The restaurant looked superb. But in the first three months of the year business tailed away to nothing (except for Friday and Saturday nights, which were full to bursting) and I was losing almost a grand a week.

Easter came and business perked up a bit, but by August with the summer holidays and all it was as flat as a pancake again. Come September a worried bank manager turned up to tell me my overdraft now stood at nearly forty thousand, and what the hell was I doing? I told him about the improvements and all and he said, yes, it was looking good. Certainly the equity was in the property OK, and the bank could support it. I think the manager was too kind – he should have shut me down six months before. Hindsight is a great thing. But with him off my back I plunged on regardless – cooking the best I could and giving the customers the best time possible. In my heart I knew I was headed for the rocks, but I just put on more sails, squared my shoulders and carried on.

If I hadn't been so stubborn I would have realized that my restaurant had become a gastronomic *Marie Celeste*. Micawber-like I thought things would improve. They did not. Christmas came and went with the usual office parties failing to turn up and leaving the place half-empty day after day. In January it snowed so badly the road was inaccessible for nearly three weeks. I opened, but nobody came.

Easter again and the terrace was bright with flowers and the exterior freshly painted. The brass door and furniture were brightly polished and the windows clean, and we hit another purple patch. Packed night after night. Things were really moving.

This was the fifth year of the restaurant. We'd had good reviews in food guides and magazines, surely I was over the hump. I planned to build a conservatory over the terrace which would give me an extra fifteen covers, but the planning officer turned it down. This grotty little street turned out to be a conservation area. I argued a Victorian conservatory would only improve things. He said not. And without the extra space I was screwed.

CHAPTER 9

I AM A CAMERA

The VAT man calls for a Routine Check. The Man from the BBC charges in looking for Soul Food and a Place to eat. Our Hero begins to wonder if he is a Chef or merely a Figment of David Pritchard's Imagination.

FOR THE LAST TWO DAYS A MILD-MANNERED, GREY LITTLE man had been going through my accounts from the last four years, sitting on table six, surrounded by untidy piles of invoices, till rolls and bank statements. His thin fingers danced on a calculator and he marked tiny figures in pencil on a sheet of foolscap paper. He was from HM Customs and Excise, carrying out an arbitrary and routine check on my VAT returns. Nothing sinister or abnormal about it. *'Purely routine'*, he said. I said, sure, help yourself, and gave him the cardboard boxes that I used as an office, and with a clear conscience carried on with my work. I was still smarting about the planning decision and I was mentally sticking pins into a wax effigy of the little runt when the phone rang.

'Keith Floyd's restaurant, can I help you?'

'Hi, it's me. I've got a great idea for a piece with you in RPM . . .'

'I'm sorry, who is this?'

'Me, David Pritchard. You remember, we spoke some weeks ago, there in your place, after dinner.'

'Yes, of course, sorry.'

'Do you fancy some lunch?'

We agreed to meet the next day. Another day, another lunch. I kept having futile lunches with media people and they all ended in tears. I wondered if he'd seen my performance on HTV, and decided he couldn't have, which was a relief.

I polished my brown brogues, selected my favourite bow tie, put on my trenchcoat and beetled off in my M-registered mini-van to lunch and Mr Pritchard.

At the Steak House he introduced me to Andy who had stacked, frizzy, blond hair and wore high-heeled, pointed cowboy boots, shiny black with buckles; a dour looking fellow called Steve with matted hair and donkey jacket; and a girl with flat granny shoes, ankle socks, knee length ski-pants, over which she wore a shapeless black dress and a pink, knitted bodice. Throughout lunch I didn't discover what the other three did or why they were there. And by the fifth bottle of Côtes du Rhone, I didn't really care. They called him Pritch and seemed to hang on his every word. He ate a huge T-bone steak and pinched the mushrooms from Steve's plate and laughed a lot, between chomping mouthfuls of food and talking of meals and banquets – he was obsessed with food.

He said, '*I like your mac, is it new? You must be rich. How much did it cost? Don't tell me, I'll guess.*' He closed his eyes. '*I bet it was more than £200. I'm right, aren't I?*'

I said I couldn't remember.

'*Do you like my Ray-Bans? They're very expensive too!*'

Then we talked about my shoes. David wore Doc Martens. His big moon face was greasy and pock-marked and quite flushed – he was very amusing, particularly when being sarcastic.

His big moon face was greasy and pock-marked and flushed

'When shall we do it, then?'

'Do what?'

'This cooking piece.'

'We haven't discussed it at all, what's it about?'

'Haven't you seen the programme?'

'I don't have time to watch TV.'

'Well, it's rock and roll, architecture, art, local bands and comedy.'

'Where do I come in?'

'You can cook something, we'll film it at your place.'

After a couple of rounds of Tia-Maria shandies (Tia Maria, brandy, hot coffee, sugar and cream – when it comes to temptation, David has the breaking strain of a hot Mars bar), we stumbled uncertainly into the afternoon agreeing to meet with a film crew at my restaurant the following Wednesday at nine-thirty.

'And we'll be out of your way by lunch time,' David said. *'Plenty of time for you to get ready for the evening.'*

Twice over lunch I alluded to my bit on HTV, but it was clear they knew nothing of it. Or Radio West.

Tant mieux.

There had been more changes in staff, and for the moment I had a good team with Annie and John upstairs as the mainstay and a couple of students who helped in the kitchen, plus my daytime jobs. The expensive black waistcoats the French guys wore were gathering mildew in the wine cellar – this lot wore Floyd's Restaurant T-shirts. I thought I might wear one myself when we filmed, but decided to put on a shirt and bow tie as usual.

About eight of them turned up for the filming. I dressed the kitchen and prepared my dish – rabbit sautéed, flamed in Armagnac and stewed with prunes – very early that morning.

There was a lot of talking, fetching things from cars and standing around while they blew fuses or found they'd forgotten the 'red', whatever that was, or needed new batteries for the radio mike. David talked a lot about 'two shots and MCUs', and under no circumstances could the cameraman use legs.

'Got to be hand held. Go with it and wing it.'

Finally they seemed to be ready, the lights were on and it was very hot, crowded and, for me, strangely lonely in my own kitchen. One of them was on the phone all morning and my girls who came in to lend moral support were kept busy making coffees and pouring drinks. By the time they were ready to turn over I was exhausted and empty. What with rehearsals and walk-throughs I felt I'd done it already.

Then David called, '*Quiet everyone.*'

'*OK.*'

'*Turn over.*'

'*Running.*'

'*And action.*'

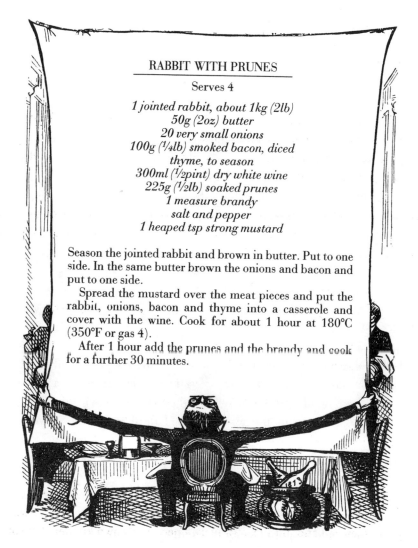

RABBIT WITH PRUNES

Serves 4

1 jointed rabbit, about 1kg (2lb)
50g (2oz) butter
20 very small onions
100g (¼lb) smoked bacon, diced
thyme, to season
300ml (½pint) dry white wine
225g (½lb) soaked prunes
1 measure brandy
salt and pepper
1 heaped tsp strong mustard

Season the jointed rabbit and brown in butter. Put to one side. In the same butter brown the onions and bacon and put to one side.

Spread the mustard over the meat pieces and put the rabbit, onions, bacon and thyme into a casserole and cover with the wine. Cook for about 1 hour at 180°C (350°F or gas 4).

After 1 hour add the prunes and the brandy and cook for a further 30 minutes.

And he nimbly, for a man of his size, tucked himself behind the
cameraman's back, slightly hunched for a better view, pursed his lips,
raised his eyebrows and nodded.

I was away, talking, chopping, gesticulating, stirring. The camera
was an extension of me, where I went it followed. I knew it was going well.

'And cut. How long?'

'Six twenty-five.'

'Good. In fact it's so good I'd like you to do it again, only this time
do it better. I know you can, you know, drop the gym mistress approach.'

I stood panting as if I'd just gone three rounds with Mohammad
Ali. One of the girls put a whisky in my hand and whispered, 'Well done'.
Luckily I had a duplicate set of ingredients and we did it again. Then I
had to mime various bits and do some 'cutaways', and the cameraman
took close-ups of the rabbit cooking, shots of me pretending to stir. Then I
had to serve the dish and be interviewed by the presenter of the programme. This turned out to be Andy.

They repeated the whole business of me nodding silently: me
talking, him nodding.

'Close up on the fork.'

The camera swung to my mouth.

'Down to the plate.'

'Two shots of Floyd and Andy.'

'And cut. Check the gate.'

'Gate clear.'

'OK, it's a wrap.'

THE WHOLE EVENT IS STILL A BLUR TO ME. I KNOW THEY ATE
a huge lunch, consumed about ten bottles of wine and had me in a state of
nervous tension for about six hours. Then they just left, leaving me empty,
feeling abused, and with the washing up. I think somebody gave me
twenty quid to cover electricity, telephones and booze, a facility fee I think
it was called. Later it occurred to me that £220 would have been more like
it.

Before he left I asked Pritchard when it would be shown.

'This week or next, I don't know.'

How could he not know? I thought. I'd just poured my heart and soul into his bloody camera and he couldn't even give me the satisfaction of knowing when it would be shown. And yet, while we were actually filming, he really seemed to care. He stayed behind the cameraman the whole time, willing me on with nods, smiles and intense stares from his big eyes.

The other strange feeling I had was that of being one with the camera. You know, each time I go into the dining room to speak to customers – human beings – I have to steel myself, even sometimes have a Scotch, before I can face them. But I felt at ease with the camera – a bloody machine for heaven's sakes – no embarrassment, no shyness. I believe I'd fallen in love with the camera.

Which was why it was so disappointing when Andy phoned to say my piece was brilliant and David was so pleased that he wanted me to do many more, but unfortunately that was the last in the series. I'd watched the programme the night before. I thought the man who played me was very good, but, you know, it wasn't really me at all. Just some figment of Pritchard's imagination, very skilfully edited. Just my luck the series had ended, I thought. Another let down. I told Andy it didn't matter to me. I'd really enjoyed taking part. And thanks very much. Inside I was as sick as a parrot.

CHAPTER 10

ANOTHER DAY OVER AND DEEPER IN DEBT

Now that the Nice Man from the VAT puts Floyd right on the finer points of Accountancy he is so Depressed he stops going to the Rugby; but finally Glimpses Salvation.

THE FOLLOWING DAY THE VAT MAN RETURNED WITH HIS 'findings'. I couldn't bring myself to listen in detail as he droned on over the columns of figures he had anotated. The bottom line was simple and brutal. I owed them £16,000, but he would not recommend I was prosecuted for fraud or anything; he could quite understand that I had attempted to calculate the VAT in my idiosyncratic way and was not being underhand. I had merely made fundamental mistakes in my accounting. Notwithstanding, it was a very serious matter indeed and the amount must be paid at once. He said he'd send a letter setting out his 'findings' in detail, by way of confirmation.

Just one of my fundamental errors, he said, was my mark up on the wine — I owed more on VAT per bottle of expensive wine than I made in profit. How come? I asked. Then it dawned on me. In my philanthropic attempts to dispense goodwill and, above all, good wines to all men I had developed a non-rip-off system for people who chose really expensive wine. Wine that cost me up to five pounds to buy, I marked up by sixty per cent, but wines that cost more than ten pounds and in some cases fifteen to twenty per bottle, I merely stuck three pounds on per bottle. Thus I made, or so I thought, about the same amount — roughly three quid a bottle — from everything I sold. Result: the customer would appreciate this and drink more wine. But in reality a bottle of wine which cost me fifteen pounds and fifteen per cent VAT, which I'd overlooked, and I sold for eighteen pounds, including VAT, was only making about thirty pence, minus the ten per cent interest the wine company charged me for being a late payer, this brought the profit down to about zero.

I thanked him and asked him not to continue the diagnosis on my food costings. Why on earth doesn't one's accountant tell you these things? I wondered, and I heard a small voice in my head say, even if he did, you wouldn't listen to him.

There was no way I could pay the VAT in time to stop the inevitable High-Court writ that would demolish my restaurant

That's another thing Mrs Thatcher must do – abolish VAT for restaurants. Must remember to write to my MP about it. Or wait till she appoints me to head the committee to sort out the tourist industry with Albert Roux.

like a child puffing at a house of cards. The restaurant continued to enjoy busy spells and many very contented customers. But I was despairing. The weeks dragged by, each morning after a sleepless night spent listening to the World Service – I never slept till 'Farming Today' – I sifted through the post for the letter from the VAT man.

Even Vin Sullivan was getting restless now and that meant the writing was on the wall. In great big capital letters. To make matters worse, the latest edition of the *Good Food Guide* came out and didn't rate me as highly as I did.

I was so pissed off in round terms I even stopped going to the rugby on Saturday afternoons. That's how low I was. Instead I'd work all Saturday morning, go to the pub till closing time and listen to the match on the local radio lying in bed, till it was time to shower and put on a bright smile for the evening. All my mates, Cuddon, Barry and all, were doing really well and shooting around the place in an assortment of fine motor cars and taking breaks in good country hotels like Gidleigh Park, or in Barry's case a quick trip to Siges, dear boy.

IN THE RESTAURANT BUSINESS YOU GET USED TO PEOPLE discovering your place, going into raptures about it, coming three times a week, spending a fortune for a couple of months and then disappearing off the face of your earth. Did they get fed-up? Did you upset them? Have they gone bankrupt? Or been arrested? Two or three big-spending customers appeared in the press awaiting fraud charges and the like. But one couple who started using the place in this way – sometimes bringing four or six guests with them – struck me as quite different from the norm. True, his dress was odd, he favoured black suits, Hawaiian shirts and pointed-toed boots. The whole ensemble was slightly too tight for his portly figure, but he, Paul, was bright and animated, and he had a beautiful wife, tall and blonde, who seemed to me to be intelligent and kind and was called Sue. They drank a lot, spent a lot and laughed a lot. Also they were very well mannered and polite towards the staff.

They'd seen me on TV, they said, and although they'd been customers of mine years ago in the old Bistro days, until that programme (of Pritchard's *and* the HTV *and* Radio West), they didn't know I was running a restaurant again.

'*You don't fool us you know,*' he said.

'Fool you? In what way?'

'*Well, your cheerful, relaxed attitude. How can you be so nice night after night? I mean those people you were talking to over there, I couldn't have been civil like you. They were peasants and bloody rude ones at that.*'

I sipped my Armagnac.

'*The other thing, old son, is you don't make any money do you? Yet you work like a dog. You need a bigger place – a big country house. Or open a chain of these and cook from a central kitchen – chill-cool vac-packed stuff – it's where the future is, old son. Mark my words.*'

'I'm not interested in restaurant chains or running empires – I had three restaurants once before and it was a nightmare.'

Sue said, '*But all the hassle with the bailiffs and the VAT, you can't live like that. I know. We had it for years. Hiding from the milkman, having the electricity cut off, selling the furniture. All that sort of thing.*'

I thought about their house in seven acres, the swimming pool, tennis court, ponies and expensive cars. I wondered what had transformed their lives.

'I could introduce you to some people, people who rate you and would be pleased to do a deal. Think about it.'

Promises at this time of night tended to be as full as the port or brandy bottle was empty.

'Let's have one for the frog and toad.'

'I do all right here you know, it's not all that bad, but more important, I'm on the side of right.'

'Bullshit,' said Paul.

There was a pale glow in the sky as they left, prelude to another fabulous September day. I wandered off to bed humming, 'Mailman bring me no more blues', and for the first time in months I slept like a log.

CHAPTER 11

IT'S ALL RIGHT MA, I'M ONLY BLEEDING

Rescued from certain Financial Ruin, thrown from the Frying Pan into the Fire of Film-Making, the cantering Cook is distressed to find he is only a Prawn in their Game.

MORNING, AND THE MAIL WAS FULL OF DOOM, GLOOM AND despondency.

HM Customs wanted their money in twenty-eight days; the bank manager requested an urgent meeting; the remainder of the letters just said ignore this demand if you have paid within the last two days — which, of course, I hadn't.

My morning meeting at the bank was negative and inconclusive, but the implications were very clear. I phoned a few estate agents and put the restaurant on the market for £95,000. If I sold it I could clear the debts and there might be enough to take a pub tenancy. The idea of a country pub with a little dining room appealed to me. Also it was the only way out. If I went bankrupt I'd not even be able to take on a pub. The idea was great. Get one with a few letting rooms as well, say, like The George in Bridport. I fancied the Devon/Somerset border, Exmoor or the Quantocks. I contacted some agents and waited excitedly for details. Ron had said he'd be quite happy to support the new venture as long as I cleared everything neatly. Looked at the other way, five years of effort was going down the pan, with no profit of any kind, but the hell with it, I was thirty-nine, just the right age to take a pub. Real Cheddar cheese, my own chutney and pickled onions, proper soups and English dishes. The scheme was great. I would no longer have to put up with people not understanding what I was doing. It would be easy.

I spent golden autumn days driving around Devon and Somerset, pub-hunting and eating exquisite lunches at The Castle in Taunton, where I sat, usually alone, dreaming of my new lifestyle. The Taunton races, a day's fishing, making potted hare and rabbit stews, and all the time the bills would be paid by people swilling beer and gin-and-tonics. At nights I cooked away cheerfully, knowing that my time in this absurd prison was nearly up.

THEN, ALMOST NINE MONTHS FROM THE TIME WE LAST MET, Pritchard phoned again.

Again the call was both detached and familiar:

'Hi, it's me. Me. David. David Pritchard. Guess what? I've got a new job. Do you want to work with me again? In Plymouth? I'll buy you lunch in Bristol tomorrow. Gotta go, there's someone in the office. Bye.'

I put down the phone feeling puzzled and curious. He phoned twice more that day and we arranged to meet in the Vittoria, a great little pub next to the BBC in Whiteladies Road, where loud rock 'n' roll from the juke box unites the stuffed birds on the wall with the bizarre mix of clientel. From BBC producers up to painters and decorators and through to temporary millionaires. You can easily tell the difference between BBC producers and painters-and-decorators: the latter don't have paint splattered all over their jeans and trainers.

David was already at the bar with three others. (I later came to realize you never met David on his own.) Steve, of the first lunch, Bernard, a big man with the face of a Viking soldier on furlough after a weekend of raping and pillaging, and another who was not introduced. From their dress I assumed they were all producers.

David ordered. *'Family-sized Scotch for Mr Floyd, please.'*

Sam dumped it on the bar with *'One large gold watch. One pound please.'*

I said 'cheers' and 'hi' to everyone. 'Hi' is very useful if you can't remember people's names, and it was many months and many meetings in the Vittoria or the BBC bar before I got Bernard and Steve's names right. They carried on talking as if I wasn't there. Evidently Bernard was just coming to the point of some in-house scandal or gossip and lowered his voice to whisper in David's ear, who put his hands on his hips, drew in a deep breath, eyes to the ceiling and burst into hysterical laughter and said, *'You're kidding! Really? Fuck my dog!'*

We lunched at Edwards restaurant and, in between setting fire to the plush velvet seats and knocking bottles of port over the tablecloth, David revealed his plan. It was for me to make a half-hour programme on cooking fish. It would be a pilot. If it was any good, we might do a whole series. The person who hadn't been introduced in the pub, but turned out to be the great Ray Gosling, did his best to sabotage Pritchard's enthusiasm by urging me to insist on an advance, clarifying the expenses and don't-be-conned-like-he'd-been so many times. All in the nicest possible way, of course. But I had no ears for that.

We left the restaurant at a quarter to five, as blood brothers. In fact we'd grown so fond of each other we helped one another into the car. Realizing the mistake I got out of the back and into the driving seat, leaving more room for Ray to have a snooze. I've not seen him from that day to this, but every time I hear his voice on the radio, so balanced, precise and modulated, probing some issue of importance, I chuckle at the memory of him on fire in a sea of port at lunch that day.

'YOU STILL HAVEN'T TOLD ME ABOUT YOUR NEW JOB,' I SAID to Pritchard.

'It's great — I've got a fridge in my office, ha, ha, ha!'

You realize very quickly when you work with Pritchard (I can't bring myself to call him Pritch) that you come very low in his list of priorities — somewhere below himself, his conception of the programme, the cameraman and the cost of film! The odd thing is, though, you don't discover what his conception of the programme *is* until he's manipulated you into some kind of performance that you didn't know you could do. He sets you a target, say to jump a four-foot fence, and having established that you can, promptly looks for a five-foot fence, and so on, till finally you stumble at eight feet. Only then does he reveal, or even decide, exactly what he's aiming for. It took me months to work this out. I was too frightened to think for myself for ages. That, and my firm belief that it's better to say nothing and be thought a fool than to open your mouth and prove beyond all doubt that you are one, prevented me from asking questions or making suggestions.

Pritchard was in full flight, commanding and countermanding

And to make matters worse. *television* has the power to trade on your insecurity. it keeps you guessing. keeps you on edge and in check. It's bigger than you. And a good director knows and will exploit that situation. just as a thoroughbred horse is aware that its rider is terrified.

When Pritchard was in full flight. commanding and countermanding, I felt like one of those little model battleships that Wrens used to push around with long sticks in the operations' room in those black-and-white war films starring people like Kenneth More. Each time one of the little ships was blown up, the admiral/director would order another one to be pushed in.

I remember little of that first shoot, but one thing that absolutely horrified me was that on the occasions when somebody did remember that we ought to stop for lunch, I suddenly realized I was now part of a gang of people, to wit a TV crew — the very same reason why I used to so dislike coming into my own restaurant. I was amazed to discover that there was no script, no prepared plan. No one told me what was expected of me. I was so ignorant of the machinations of television that I thought the stop-watch Frances (the production assistant) held was for some kind of time and motion study!

I bumbled through the first day at Sonia Stevenson's restaurant.

The Horn of Plenty, in Gunnislake, desperately trying to get it right and, after the others had unceremoniously gone home, unable to face the empty and very tatty hotel room, I sought some kind of solace in an all-night bar on Union Street, Plymouth. Watching hookers inject cocaine and night people doing deals. It was a ghastly experience, like taking part in the film version of Jean Genet's *Thieves' Journal*, directed by a lunatic. Each time I dozed off someone shook me awake till morning finally came and I ran unshaven and wrecked to meet the crew on the jetty at seven a.m.

We put to sea in a trawler on a fine morning. When we reached the fishing grounds Pritchard asked the crew to shoot the net and told me to deliver a fruity, passionate piece to camera about the sorry plight of English fish-eating habits.

'*OK, turnover.*'

'*Running.*'

'*And action.*'

I delivered what I thought was a passable piece, given that I actually had at that precise moment no views whatsoever on the sorry plight of English fish-eating habits. I certainly didn't know what a 'piece to camera' was.

The sound man complained that the noise of the engine was causing too much interference. '*Then tell them to switch the engine off,*' snapped David.

'*Then they can't winch in the net.*'

'*Not my problem. OK, let's go again. Turn over. And . . . action.*'

This went on for hours. Pritchard was getting very impatient. By take twenty he was white with rage. At me. Either my delivery was too loud (it had to be, because of the engine), or I muddled my words or I sounded like a 'News at Ten' reporter.

The crew were pissed off with me and Pritchard and kept muttering about presenters who normally need a maximum of one minute to prepare for a take and no more than three attempts to get it into the can. The crew were particularly resentful – after all they didn't know I hadn't done it before. That I was completely green. They just assumed I was hopeless. Pritchard kept worrying about the amount of useless film he'd shot. Anyone would think he had to buy it out of his own salary.

The boat's crew had been landing some fish and late in the afternoon Pritchard set up in the tiny galley with a single burner camping gas stove rolling around in a small sink and told me to cook something. I did and, despite the cramped conditions, the virtual non-existence of equipment or ingredients, did it well. With food in my hands and a lot of luck I found again the form that had so (I later learned from someone else) pleased him when I cooked the rabbit in my restaurant kitchen.

We returned to harbour with the day salvaged and got wildly pissed in the Navy or the Dolphin — I forget which — on the Barbican. Afterwards we had dinner — which consisted mainly (for me) of espresso coffees and Amarettos — David ate his and mine with relish, at the Hosteria de Romana which we renamed Hysteria de Romana.

Pritchard managed to switch the blame of the disaster from me to the film crew. It was a transparent act of insincerity on his part, but it was his way of saying, well done mush. You hacked it in the end.

The shoot finished in the Plymouth shopping centre as abruptly as it had begun, three (was that all?) days earlier.

Pritchard said,

'Great, that's a wrap, bye.'

It was 1983, I was forty years old but felt like I was fifteen and had flunked a match-saving tackle that disgraced the entire school.

CHAPTER 12

I SHALL BE RELEASED

New friendships with the Sun and Jupiter in conjunction will give you the Opportunity to make lots of Money and Live Happily Ever After. Lucky colour: Green.

BACK IN BRISTOL I REALIZED THAT MY RESTAURANT, RATHER than a mad merry-go-round of mayhem, was, after the last manic days during which I felt as though I'd lived the part of the Marquis de Sade in the Asylum of Charenton, an ordered and calm place, and I was glad to be back, even though, despite my detailed instructions and my staff's assurances to the contrary, the unexpected had happened. The electricity had blown and it took them a day and a half to get it fixed with the resulting loss in business. Which only fired speculation then rife that I was about to go under.

Sue and Paul were still regular customers and we'd become very friendly. I think they were even more excited about the film than I, and Paul demanded to have a copy of the video at the earliest opportunity. When Pritchard sent me a cassette of the rough cut they came at once to see it. And although I couldn't watch it (though, of course, I did) they thought it brilliant and took it away to make a copy. I said, 'Don't forget it'll be better when the commentary is dubbed on – don't show it to anyone without explaining that.' He wanted to show it to someone who'd be very interested in it. And Paul, now that he had sold his business for some vast sum to an Arab, was getting bored and had a great idea.

'What sort of idea?' I asked.

'*Don't worry old son, leave it to me.*'

As they left Sue whispered, '*Do as he says, leave it to him.*'

Then the weather broke with an electric storm of such awesome power that I really thought the roof of the restaurant would be blown in. The window boxes were flattened, the shrubs and trees on the terrace were destroyed and my kitchen, through some quirk of blinding malpractice, was a foot deep in rainwater. I, in my usual cheerful way, was fumbling around with a manhole cover, wondering what to do. It's very difficult to think about draining the swamp when you are up to your balls in alligators! It was quite a funny scene actually, chopping-boards and wooden spoons drifting by, when I received two telephone calls within five minutes of each other that were to alter my life dramatically.

First Pritchard phoned to say that 'they' were so pleased with the fish programme they wanted to make a series. And Paul phoned to say he wanted to buy my restaurant.

I called Cuddon – I needed to talk through this lot with someone, and he had an entrepreneurial way of looking at things. The occasion seemed to call for a serious lunch, so we went to a very famous and expensive restaurant just outside London. You have to understand that whenever I go to one of these grand places, it's a disaster, which only serves to reinforce my dim view of the British restaurant business.

After the usual preliminaries – getting the waiter to take the lemon slices out of the water, put ice into Cuddon's aperitif, add water to mine, bring some clean cutlery and fresh butter – things proceeded rather well.

A chip on Cuddon's glass caused a temporary hiccup in our pally relations with the waiter, but the *foie gras* and the toast met with our approval. True, the lamb's tongue salad garnish was rusty at the edges and the *confiture d'oignons* was a little greasy, but we graciously let this be.

My main course of grilled rabbit fillets stacked like the framework for a log cabin was a delight, but unfortunately and, I suppose, inevitably, Cuddon's kidneys *aigre-doux* were leathery and caramelized and had to be rejected. The waiting staff united against us in defence of the kitchen, but finally lost about fifteen to three when the chef emerged to explain and replace the dish. The *Château Grillet* was supreme, and the *Condrieu* tasted rich, vermilion and slightly burned. It was just the same, first-class. For a change the *mange tout* had been stripped, but I dislike them anyway. The cheese was average, but the raspberry soufflé was out of this world. All up, with first-class rail fares, taxi and tip, lunch cost about three hundred pounds for two. '*Next time we have lunch,*' Cuddon said, reaching for the cognac bottle that our host had kindly left on the table, '*Let's make it Paris.*'

'So let's get this straight. He's going to buy the restaurant with a company, which enables you to clear your debts and have cash over to get a mortgage on a house; you get shares in the company, plus a service contract for an annual amount. You put your name to the satellite units and oversee the food and design concepts. Right?'

'That's right. But the point is do you actually believe it all?'

'Well, it matches with what he's told me so I think yes. I reckon you've cracked it.'

'I'll drink to that.'

ON DECEMBER 28 I THREW A PARTY FOR THE FIFTH AND FINAL anniversary of the restaurant and my birthday. The *Evening Post* carried a story headlined, 'Floyd sells out for a fast duck', which I thought was very funny, and my lawyer explained to my creditors that they'd all be paid by the end of February. The die was cast. I dropped my pub plans and set about house-hunting instead. And looked forward to 1984 with relish.

PART TWO

CHAPTER 13

CAROUSEL

The Roundabout gathers speed. Floyd finds himself pursued by Fans and Creditors alike; Personal tragedy and the Machinations of Bureaucracy leave him Down. But absolutely Not Out.

AFTER CHRISTMAS THE RESTAURANT BUSINESS HAS ALWAYS been, for me, a grim time: massive bills, bad gloomy weather, draughty dining rooms, windows running with condensation, and poor business. But January 1985 was quite different; my spirits were very high. I toddled around the place with a song in my heart and a spring in my step. The once-loved restaurant which had finally become a gastronomic coalface where, it seemed, I toiled in the dark only to start each day deeper in debt, was closed. The relief was extraordinary. For some time I could not sleep before my habitual 2 or 3 a.m., but now it was excitement that kept me awake, not anxiety. Having the days free to contemplate the juicy future that would unfold when Paul's cheque finally wiped out the creditors *and* we had bought a new house gave me the feeling I should think a man wrongly imprisoned has when he's told his appeal has been successful. Not only all this but I was also about to start a TV series as well.

Despite the howling winds and the driving rain I could not see a cloud in the sky as I drove down the M5 to meet David Pritchard and his assistant, Frances, at Penzance. It was night when I arrived and black rain swirled along the bleak pavements. The hotel was desolate, with cream paint, garish carpets and no other guests. We ate in the only open restaurant and after dinner a lady read tarot cards for me which assured me of great success. But she said that once I had achieved it I would tire of this success and seek shelter in some quiet place where, as a late developer, I would find true happiness with a woman who, she said alarmingly, was not the one I was married to at the time. She said I had a driving ambition, remarkable tenacity and an ability to cope with hurt

and disappointment – '*Two companions that are not strangers to you.*'
     She said much more that I can't tell you.
     The next morning we were at the fish quay in Newlyn to film the
market where I had to buy some fish to make a stew. The fishermen took
the piss out of me unmercifully as I tried to walk up and down the quay
without my knees knocking. Why they found the thing so funny was
beyond me till Frances noticed that they'd pinned a notice to my back
saying 'Floyd is a prick'. But I had my revenge when they gathered to hear
me do a piece to camera which involved indicating the poisonous spine on
a weaver fish. 'Take care of the pricks,' I said, 'there are a lot of them
about.' The fishermen roared. I suppose in a way they were now prepared
to give me a chance.
     I can tell you it takes nerve to mince up and down a fish quay at
seven in the morning swinging a shopping bag and apparently talking to
yourself in front of a bunch of hairy-arsed fishermen. Anyway, I must
have had it because they were very generous in the pub afterwards. (Some
months later after 'Fish' had been transmitted locally in the South West I
bumped into the Newlyn cricket team in Dorset – they greeted me as if I'd
won the test match single-handed and forced drinks down me till I could
barely stand.)
     The weeks went by in a rain-sodden wind-blown blur, leaping on
and off fishing boats, cooking in impossibly small galleys and bursting
into restaurants whose owners believed a ten-minute sequence would only
take half an hour – of course we were there all day, tramping in and out,
switching off their fridges and telling the staff to be quiet. David, dictatorial and dizzy, directed from bollards on a quay or crouched in a locker
of some trawler. Always stopping too soon or too late for lunch. Cold,
out-of-season hotels usually without restaurants became our homes for
weeks on end and the sun seldom shone.
     Although I was exhausted by long hours and the uncertainty of
where or what we'd be doing next, I was having the time of my life. No
matter that the fee I was being paid for seven programmes was appallingly low – I really didn't care. To hell with the money. To hell with the
measly meal allowances: it was just the break I needed – the chance to do
something new that seemed to come naturally and that I seemed to be
rather good at. What was really pleasing was that the years and years I'd
been slaving away at stoves and the years and years I'd been giving myself
ulcers and a bad liver by eating too many different meals in too many

different countries was now proving to be really useful. And I didn't even have to rehearse: I knew enough about food to do it straight off the top of my head!

In Ric Stein's Seafood Restaurant in Padstow I cooked shark and called him Charles — even though I'd known him for years — and David left it in. In Weymouth I waded for cockles that weren't there up to my knees in freezing water till David got the shot he wanted of some windsurfers crisscrossing behind me. I froze for six hours on a pilchard drifter and with numb fingers hand-hauled in the net that yielded not three tons of pilchards as the fishermen had promised but just three fish. They, of course, blamed our misfortune on Frances. *'Shouldn't have a maid on board'*, they muttered. The three fish we caught I charcoal-grilled on the Newlyn quay on a small portable barbecue that (much to the delight of the incredulous knot of spectators who wondered what the hell we were doing cooking fish at 10.30 in the middle of a winter's night) David, in his rush to get to the pub, knocked into the water.

I was water-bombed as I tried to cook a fish soup on board the *Pelican* by the other boats in the annual Plymouth Trawler race. Made to

eat oysters till I was almost sick on the Barbican steps while David toyed with the idea of me doing a fruity, passionate and philosophical piece about the Pilgrim Fathers. The item was never used. On the Somerset levels on a frosty March morning with the bare trees shrouded in mist I landed a huge pike and the next day to the fury of Pritchard lost a large (and the only) salmon on the River Exe where he had me wading for several hours I'm sure as a punishment.

David directed well, though his temper was short, and boredom or disappointment were always close behind. But once the day's filming was over the nights

were usually good fun, and over endless pints we'd thrash out the plan
for tomorrow. We never had a script (we still don't and never will)
which amazed me the first time, but Pritchard and I, though we are
so completely different in every way, seem to have some strange ability
to spark off each other and create programmes from nothing. Usually
the only thing we know for certain before we start is what rough

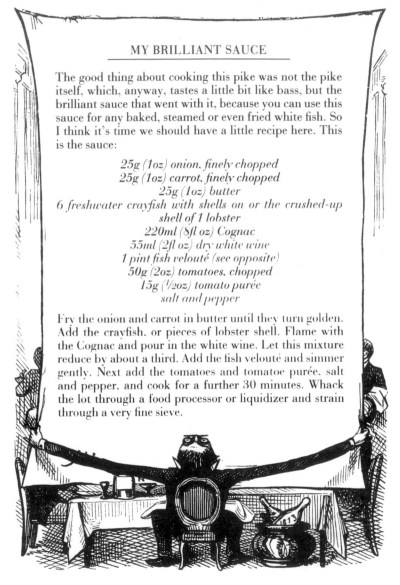

MY BRILLIANT SAUCE

The good thing about cooking this pike was not the pike
itself, which, anyway, tastes a little bit like bass, but the
brilliant sauce that went with it, because you can use this
sauce for any baked, steamed or even fried white fish. So
I think it's time we should have a little recipe here. This
is the sauce:

25g (1oz) onion, finely chopped
25g (1oz) carrot, finely chopped
25g (1oz) butter
6 freshwater crayfish with shells on or the crushed-up
shell of 1 lobster
220ml (8fl oz) Cognac
55ml (2fl oz) dry white wine
1 pint fish velouté (see opposite)
50g (2oz) tomatoes, chopped
15g (½oz) tomato purée
salt and pepper

Fry the onion and carrot in butter until they turn golden.
Add the crayfish. or pieces of lobster shell. Flame with
the Cognac and pour in the white wine. Let this mixture
reduce by about a third. Add the fish velouté and simmer
gently. Next add the tomatoes and tomato purée. salt
and pepper, and cook for a further 30 minutes. Whack
the lot through a food processor or liquidizer and strain
through a very fine sieve.

After dinner, the place looked like a battlefield.

I loved the dining room empty – fine, white, and uncluttered, with vivid splashes of colour from the cut flowers.

*Life, like fishing, is full of snags;
and sometimes the most well-
executed cast will result in the
hook becoming firmly lodged in
your ear.*

*'Let's have a fruity, passionate piece
to camera about the sorry plight of
English fish-eating habits.'*

Pritchard as Chabrol, me as Alain Delon.

'If anyone were to write an epitaph for Keith Floyd it would have to be that he was the only foodie who was never afraid to fart.'

CHRISTOPHER CHAPMAN

geographical area we'll be in and what I'll (most likely) be cooking.

Some time during this whirlwind tour of the West Country's fishing ports the crew changed and Clive North, Andy McCormack and Tim White became the regular team – much to David's delight, not least because of their professionalism but also because of their creative input into the programmes. And also, I suspect, because he was beginning to tire

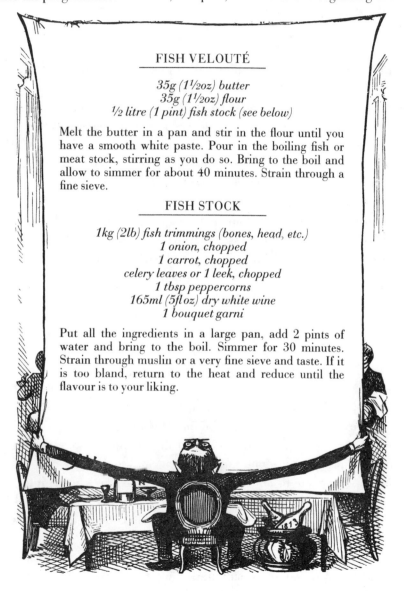

FISH VELOUTÉ

35g (1½oz) butter
35g (1½oz) flour
½ litre (1 pint) fish stock (see below)

Melt the butter in a pan and stir in the flour until you have a smooth white paste. Pour in the boiling fish or meat stock, stirring as you do so. Bring to the boil and allow to simmer for about 40 minutes. Strain through a fine sieve.

FISH STOCK

1kg (2lb) fish trimmings (bones, head, etc.)
1 onion, chopped
1 carrot, chopped
celery leaves or 1 leek, chopped
1 tbsp peppercorns
165ml (5fl oz) dry white wine
1 bouquet garni

Put all the ingredients in a large pan, add 2 pints of water and bring to the boil. Simmer for 30 minutes. Strain through muslin or a very fine sieve and taste. If it is too bland, return to the heat and reduce until the flavour is to your liking.

of having to talk to me at dinner times. Frances and an occasional lighting man made up the team of seven of us in all.

Sometimes, if we were filming near enough to Plymouth, I'd stay with Frances and her husband Terry at Saltash. During those months this was the nearest I ever got to a home life and Frances' breakfasts were brilliant and generous.

UNBEKNOWN TO ME THERE WERE PEOPLE AT BROADCASTING House in Plymouth who felt resentful about our series and this made David very secretive about what we were doing. This, of course, irritated me because I thought the more people who knew of it the better chance it would have of a possible network-showing. I began to wonder whether it would be shown at all, never mind networked. Rumours flew round the building that the programme was crappy and completely over the top and unshowable. This depressed me deeply and infuriated me at the same time, for I knew it wasn't true and I wanted David to go out and 'sell' it to all his colleagues. Since then I've learnt that his great strength is creative programme-making, not the infighting and wheeling-and-dealing neces-sary to exploit or even transmit the finished article. In fact it sometimes seems he has no interest in a programme outside of making it. Like being overjoyed at having a baby then leaving it on the steps of a church.

THE FILMING OF 'FLOYD ON FISH' CONTINUED, A BIZARRE MIX of gut-busting hilarity, heartache and headaches, seriousness and profes-sional levity that was definitely sobering. One thing we all became very proud of was that despite the rows and the hiccups, despite appalling weather, impossible locations and a parsimonious budget, we could turn round a programme in about four days. Everybody put more into the shoot – it was as if we were raiders behind enemy lines and we had to knock out the guards, snatch the gold and get back to base before dawn. You know the scenario?

In January David had briefly mentioned that BBC Publications (now BBC Books) had expressed interest in a book to go with the series, but the months had passed and I'd heard nothing and decided it had just been some kind of sop to make me feel good. So I phoned BBC Publications and, of course, they knew nothing about it. I say 'of course' not because of anything specific, but because it was beginning to dawn on me that the right hand did not always know or perhaps even care what the left was doing. Whether all of this was some kind of carrot or a stick I couldn't work out. And David would never admit or deny any real knowledge of what was going on. *'I only make the monkies, mush. The BBC decides the rest,'* he said, as if he wasn't a part of it.

I was despondent to say the least. Then I remembered Jon Croft. He'd be certain to want to publish the book. When I called him he was cautious and although he didn't say no, he suggested that he write to BBC Publications at least to give them the opportunity, before making a final decision himself. The reply was immediate. Please come to London at once.

At lunch Roger Chown, then BBC Publications' marketing director, and the editor, Susan Kennedy, expressed enormous interest in a *Floyd on Fish* book and said could they have it no later than the middle of May. About six weeks later. 'You bet,' I said. Jon Croft said he'd like to be involved as the editor – since he'd first published me and Absolute Press would be 'in association' with the BBC and he'd take a slice of my percentage. Not a bad deal for him as it turned out – the book sold about two hundred thousand copies. Anyway, I was quite happy and I reckoned it meant he owed me one. I think that Roger and Susan's faith and enthusiasm in that first book has been the most important single factor in the success that I have enjoyed since making the pilot programme for 'Fish'. Not only have they been able to inject money into my other series, they also encouraged me to carry on at times when the curious happenings on high made me want to quit.

No sooner did I have the contract for my book than I heard the plan to buy my restaurant and with it the whole franchise deal was off. After weeks of assuring me each day that he'd give me the money tomorrow Paul finally admitted that he hadn't any money. I was devastated. I'd promised my creditors payment in full – my solicitor had indeed written to them all promising these payments. Now our house was in danger of being seized by at least the bank. It was horrible. It ruined everything. The bailiffs were back in force and threatening letters arrived in flurries.

Roger Chown temporarily stayed my financial execution by

paying me a generous advance on royalties. It was the largest cheque payable to me I'd ever seen. And I glimpsed it for only a few seconds before I signed it on the back and handed it to my solicitor to distribute the money amongst the clamouring creditors. That was September 85. I managed finally to clear the rest by April 87. Two years' sodding hard work. It would have been impossible on TV fees alone, but I did it through books and personal appearances and with the managerial ability of my manager John Miles.

So between recce-ing filming and fending off creditors I set about writing *Floyd on Fish*. Pritchard lent me an office at the Beeb and I cracked on with it. I was halfway through, with the time running out, when Dad died. The bloody door just shut again. My sister Brenda and I did what we could to comfort Mum. I was too numbed by so many awful twists of fortune to register my own loss at the time – that came later when I realized that this gentle kind and intelligent man would never have the satisfaction (that I am pleased to say mum has enjoyed) of his son 'getting on'. I hope that doesn't sound selfish but I know he'd have got one hell of a kick out of it. I was glad we had been close and that we'd had happy drinks and meals together. Just on our own. But I miss him. Specially at Christmas when he'd get pissed and sing wonderful carols.

THAT SUMMER 'FLOYD ON FISH' WAS SCREENED IN THE SOUTH West with the promise of a network showing in the autumn to coincide with the publication of the book in November. We finished filming in St Malo and by now I was heartily sick of fish! So I was thrilled to bits when Mike Read (Regional TV Manager, Plymouth) gave David the go ahead for another (regional) series to be called 'Floyd on Food'. Whizzing round the West Country again, but easy on the fish. This time we shot on video with the now famous Richard Elliott, Dave Manford, Mike Foren and Richard Davies. Having just got used to working with film I now had to learn a whole new technique and, more worryingly, so did David. He hated video and sulked like someone who's lost a pound and found sixpence.

To our intense relief and not little amazement 'Floyd on Fish' went down a storm in the West Country and fan letters poured in by their thousands. We were already working on another series and my solicitor, armed with that and the book and a good line in confidence-instilling chat, was keeping the creditors at bay. Things were going fairly smoothly when the bloody door slammed again. The 'Programme Planners' announced that 'Floyd on Fish' would not now be networked until March 86. When I told Susan Kennedy this she went egg-shaped. How could one arm of the BBC make this kind of decision without informing the other? The book was irrevocably planned for November, but without the TV series it would bomb and there'd be no chance of earning the money they'd already given me.

I'd often been in the soup, as Bertie Wooster used to say, but now I was up to my neck in it.

It took about two weeks to get the planners' decision reversed and things back on schedule. But during that awful time a big slice of innate faith that I've always tried to cling to died in me. The last eighteen months had seesawed so; I was dizzy.

With the network screening of 'Fish' and the national recognition that came in its wake so came endless outings to restaurants with book publishers, magazine editors, ad agencies and TV producers, when it was always assumed that I'd like to eat fish. And I said, yes, I would. Sometimes I'd have given my right arm for a hamburger.

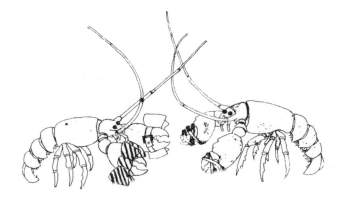

"It's always been my
ambition to be on Floyd's programme!"

14th September 1987

Dear Keith

My wife and I regularly holiday in that heaven on earth, France, and we
also want to leap about with enthusiasm a la Floyd when we see the food
on display in French markets. Strangely, this delight for things
gastronomique seems unable to communicate itself to the majority of our
fellow Brits. I had begun to despair of finding someone else in this world
who could be sent into raptures by the simple pleasures of French food and
wine - until you came along with your TV programme.

Could you possibly give me a receipe for those magnificent dishes which
are displayed in the charcuterie - in particular Champignons a la Grecque
and Celeri a la Remoulade. I am unable to pass a window displaying these
delights without picking up a couple of 200 gramme parcels. An old receipe
book suggested an a la Grecque sauce with white spirit vinegar, but the
resulting mess nearly took the roof of my mouth off. In any case it wasn't
a bit like the real thing. Une Francaise explained to me that the Celeri
is made from a tete forced through a Mouli Julienne, but are these roots
available in the UK?

An SAE is enclosed for your reply. Keep being nice to Clive, he does
wonders with that camera in the confined, oil-splashing kitchens in which
you confine him.

Regards,

Charles Mercer

Charles Mercer

February 1987

Dear Mr. Floyd,
    I am not going to beat about the bush,
I am going to come straight out with
it... will you please marry me? It's
not that much to ask for, is it? Such
a simple little request, all you have to
say is "yes"!
    But, unknown to I, you may already
be married. No problem. I'll settle for a
hot, passionate affair with you (that
sounds more fun than getting married
come to think about it - yes, let's have
an affair!)

Mr. Keith Floyd
c/o BBC TV Centre
Wood Lane
London W1R 8QT

Dear Mr Floyd,

your programmes on BBC2 were, in my opinion, brilliant, especially "Floyd on France." - Seeing you and in action has made me consider becoming a chef myself, so I would be grateful if you could send me some information about becoming a chef, such as qualifactions, for example.

Cooking has only just become an interest of mine. I do, of course, have my critics, but, as I keep saying, all the best chefs are men!

Thank you very much,

Yours Sincerely,

Matthew Levy
(aged 15)

10/3/87

Dear Floyd,

We have just seen your final Floyd on Food Etc. Read-on = don't IGNORE! Thank's Exellant viewing and without to much Pyrotechnicality you are such an Efficacious Effervesant congenial forcible-Gentle botargo congere beverage supping friendly charming No nonsense Angelic gastronomic cherub of Real "mature" cookinghood! Believe it, you can say "Borridge" to us lot here in Australia any Time We have not missed one of your "Floyd's," good quality mate, and when you finally Run-out of ideas -come to Australia mate, Witchy Grub Soup, Kangeroo with mint sauce or Try our fried Ants Floyd you are positively Audacious to Reverie, we love you and Enjoy your style! Please another and more floyds, we shall always miss you, slurp, slurp, please do Reply or say Hello
          God bless
          Michael e family

Dear Mr Floyd

Firstly, I must tell you how much I enjoy your television
programmes which I have watched from the outset. I am
particularly enjoying the current series in France.

However (and here comes the "nitty-gritty") although I have
successfuly tried an earlier recipe of yours (shown on the
T.V.) I must tell you of the complete disaster I had with the
Auvergne Cherry Cake detailed in the Sunday Express magazine
several weeks ago.

On the one occasion when I actually followed a recipe exactly,
including weighing every ingredient, the result was a complete
failure! The cake turned out looking like a flat pancake and
tasted awful!!! What did I do wrong?

It did give everyone a good laugh, so I suppose all was not
lost.

I should very much appreciate your comments in due course and
wonder whether anyone else has written to you in this matter.

I look forward to hearing from you.

Yours truly

Shirley Lewis (Mrs.)

IN EARLY 86 JON CROFT ASKED ME TO WRITE A BARBECUE
book, *Floyd on Fire*, which he was able to co-publish with BBC Publications in May of the same year. Pritchard and I carried on shooting
'Floyd on Food' while Susan, Roger and I were planning a *Floyd on
France* book, which would mean David would have the money to shoot
the series which would go straight on to the network in autumn 87. I
finished shooting the 'Food' series, and did a quick nationwide tour to
promote *Fire* before leaving for France to start shooting in July. In
between times John Miles was filling any empty spaces with personal
appearances, radio shows, commercials, cookery demonstrations and
speeches. I was writing for *The Sunday Times* and other magazines until
the *Sunday Express* offered me an exclusive contract which I accepted
happily. Working for Dee Nolan and Michael Bateman on that paper can
only be described as a pleasure, with plenty of intervals for far-reaching
editorial planning meetings usually held in an agreeable restaurant of my
choice. Life's not so bad, really, is it? If you don't weaken.

CHAPTER 14

THE BEGGARS' BANQUET

A gastronomic Cascade that is jeopardized by Acts of God, Electricity Cuts, Balloon Crashes and a very slight Difference of Opinion with the Man From The BBC.

THE NIGHT SKY IS THE DEEP TRANSLUCENT BLUE OF BRISTOL glass. On the wide pavement under the plantains the tables are full with noisy diners scoffing *brochettes, merguez, andouillette* and chops. Tanned kids with slicked-back hair, white T-shirts and medallions sit calling and whistling on their brightly coloured motorbikes, revving the punctured exhausts to screaming point. Across the road under the dark shadows of the trees – their silver trunks disappearing into the night – the river Sorgue flows swift, black and cold.

Lights and shadows from the balconies of the building on the far side of the river dance and flicker in the murmuring current. A man in his vest leans over the wrought-iron balustrade of his balcony and watches the world drift by. I can hear his TV clearly. I play with the gravel – doodling with my espadrilles. The night is very warm. The cook throws a pinch of fried herbs on to his charcoal grill and sweet-smelling sparks shoot like fireflies into the night. And die. The Arab kid comes for my order. I want to drink Pastis, then to eat *brochettes* of beef heart and drink a litre of iced rosé – of a colour between that of a pale rose and an onion skin. The boy comes back with strong mustard, *harissa*, bread, salt and pepper, my drinks and a carafe of water. The cook sweats over the hot grill and his wife waits hands on hips, black hair pulled tight into a bun, to dish up the food. Council workers in jeans are hanging lights between the trees. Others are building a stage across the river.

Fly posters on trees and windows proclaim dances, lotto and feasts. Provence is preparing for the fourteenth of July, when bands will play and fireworks explode in glorious celebration of the French Revolution. An old man with two white mongrels tethered to his feet is sleeping off the booze at a table by the door. When he wakes the locals will send him home. Saying, no more tonight. But he'll be there again tomorrow. And the next night, I suppose, until the Pastis or a juggernaut gets him.

In three days' time we start filming 'Floyd on France'. For me it's the big one. And to make things even better we're starting in the small village where I used to live, L'Isle sur la Sorgue. It was like coming home.

When I lived there, I'm sure the locals used to think I was completely mad, but they treated me like some kind of ambassador. For example, when the pound was devalued it was my fault; when England failed once again to win a match against France in the Five Nations

Sometimes when I wasn't doing too well Leo would take me out for lunch

Championship, I was the one with whom they commiserated; on the day Mountbatten was murdered it took me eight minutes to make it to the market place for my shopping because each person in the street said, we are sorry for you that Mountbatten has been killed, because, you see, for the French he was the last of the great war leaders.

So it was a joy to get back into Leo's bar and have a few Pastis and watch the old men playing *bullotte*, which is a kind of card game which still mystifies me, but they get very passionate about it as they sit there in their carpet slippers, leather flying jackets and sort of tartan flat caps, whispering and passing drinks to each other. It was good to see Leo too. His second name was Grimm. He was from the Alsace region where lots of Grimms came from and he was a kind, nice man. Sometimes in the old days, when I wasn't doing too well he would take me out for lunch or maybe give me a fish.

It was like coming home

We had a brilliant film crew with us in France. Clive North, the principal cameraman, is thoroughly professional, and after dinner when the brandy talks he keeps his own counsel. Clive used to get up early every morning to get what he called the 'pretties' – the wonderful shots that give the programmes their third dimension of fresh air and interest.

Andy McCormack, the assistant cameraman, is relaxed and gentle – a child of the sixties with a vast knowledge of literature, rock-and-roll and a great interest in food.

John Clifton, the sound guy, was totally at ease in France, well travelled, self-sufficient and calm. Steve Williams, the lighting man, flamboyant, theatrical, incredibly hard-working and very kind and extremely funny in a self-deprecating way, completed the team.

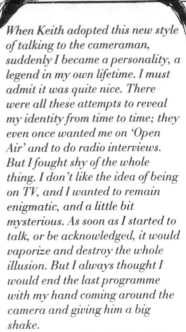

Clive keeps his own counsel

When Keith adopted this new style of talking to the cameraman, suddenly I became a personality, a legend in my own lifetime. I must admit it was quite nice. There were all these attempts to reveal my identity from time to time; they even once wanted me on 'Open Air' and to do radio interviews. But I fought shy of the whole thing. I don't like the idea of being on TV, and I wanted to remain enigmatic, and a little bit mysterious. As soon as I started to talk, or be acknowledged, it would vaporize and destroy the whole illusion. But I always thought I would end the last programme with my hand coming around the camera and giving him a big shake.

CLIVE NORTH

Clive was up early every morning getting what he called 'the pretties'

Steve, the lighting man, hard at work as usual

Andy – a child of the sixties

There was one time when we had driven from Provence up to Perigord. It was a twelve-hour drive, and everyone, Keith included, was knackered. Pritch had declared a day off to recover, and so I took a crew car and drove down to Bergerac at lunchtime, to get away and have a look around the town. I got myself something to eat and suddenly I couldn't find the car. It got to the point where I went to the tourist board and got a map from them to do a grid search. I just couldn't find it. I wandered about for three hours, I knew it was there somewhere, but I couldn't speak a word of French and couldn't find anyone who spoke English – I didn't even know which hotel we were in. I went back to the tourist office, found someone who spoke English and eventually got through to the hotel and located Keith who was not in a particularly good mood. He was sitting on his own in the restaurant, eating some disgustingly expensive dish like freshwater crayfish which cost him an arm and a leg, and there I was on the phone saying I couldn't get back because I'd lost the car . . . His langoustine went cold and he was not very pleased.

Eventually, he said wait until Pritch gets back and we'll come and get you. Then I looked out of the window and saw the car 100 yards away from me. I couldn't believe it. I rang back half an hour later and told him. He wasn't furious, he was highly amused. He thought I was a complete moron.

ANDY McCORMACK

Andy, the only reason I was in a bad mood was that a few minutes before you called me David and the cameraman had rung to say they'd run out of petrol and would I bring them some. And when I arrived I had to lend them some money to pay for the drinks they had ordered in the meantime.

Keith

Pritchard is directing extremely well. Hunched like a crow behind Clive's shoulder, urging me, willing me on

IN ALSACE, IN THE MUNSTER VALLEY WHERE MUNSTER cheese is made from the creamy milk of cows that wear bells and live on the pine-covered slopes of a Julie Andrews' film set, I was invited to lunch with some farmers. I accepted with alacrity. Visions of steaming plates of *choucroute* washed down with buckets of Alsace Riesling were swimming through my brain.

All such thoughts were abruptly dispelled when my director had one of his brilliant ideas . . . *'Why don't we,'* he said, *'film you arriving at the farm by balloon? It would be very funny,'* he assured me, promising wonderful shots for the opening titles.

'No it wouldn't,' I said.

'It wouldn't what?' he asked.

'Be very funny,' I said.

'Why?'

'I don't like balloons,' I informed him. 'And, anyway, I'm not insured for stunt work.'

'Of course you are. Isn't he?'

'Well, yes. He is.'

'Well, I'm still not going,' I said finally.

To my horror, the following morning dawned.clear and golden. I had prayed for fog and mist, but a perfect sun shone brightly on the ripe vines. God was in heaven. My heart was in my boots — suede brogues, actually. The balloon climbed slowly into the still morning air as the ground film crew waved. It kept climbing till I became quite dizzy looking over the side of the ridiculous laundry basket that was transporting me up, up and away. Oh, God. To the sound of my hiccups and tummy rumblings the cameraman chatted happily to the pilot, a puck-like figure in a natty red flying suit. I had to pray for deliverance.

Well, my dear gastronauts, the inevitable happened. The damned balloon crashed. I didn't get my lunch ... In fact, we didn't even get rescued for some considerable time as the ground crew had managed to get lost or bored or both and had adjourned to the bar for a little livener. Needless to say, the director was furious that we hadn't been filming as we actually crashed. *'Would have made a brilliant sequence. Bloody shame.'* I was furious, not about the filming, but about the heartless lack of concern for my health. I lost my temper. We didn't speak for a day or two. However, as a way of apology, he gallantly offered to take me out for lunch at the Maison des Têtes in Colmar.

The inevitable happened . . .

ONE DAY WE WERE SITTING IN A BAR IN BURGUNDY ENJOYING
some very large glasses of Kir Cardinal, made from double strength *Crème
de Cassis* and heady Gevrais Chambertin in Madame Le Clerc's elegant
hotel, when she said, gazing at her vividly painted red fingernails and
smoothing down the front of her leather frock, that tomorrow the worst
fortnight of her year was to start. Tomorrow with the *vendange*, thirty-
odd grape-pickers would arrive, who three times a day, at breakfast,
lunch and dinner – the most important of these was lunch – had to be fed
with fine but substantial food. Why, she said, she had ever married her
husband in general and why she had married a wine grower in particular,
she would never know.

To have her house invaded by these frightful people was just too
much and if there was one thing she really loathed it was cooking. I should
have known something was wrong, something was in the air, some sinister
orchestration of fate was taking place, when I noticed my director paying
rapt attention to Madame's outburst. So moved was he that he ordered
and paid for another round of these highly expensive Kirs. A strange glow
shone on his face. His round eyes shone like stars in his pale moon face.
'*Do you know what I'm thinking, Floyd?*' he said.

I felt a cold shudder, that sense of chill that you get whilst lying
with your neck exposed on a silk-sheeted bed and you hear the familiar
flap of leather wings and look up and find Christopher Lee smiling at you.
Yes, I knew only too well what he was thinking. I was to cook the first
lunch for the grape-pickers.

We decided on a menu of *crudités*, things like grated celeriac with
home-made mayonnaise, tuna-fish and tomato salads tossed in olive oil
and basil. Rice and ham, mounds of pink, hot radishes served with
squares of butter, rich pork pâté, etc., etc. The classic dish of Burgundy,
chicken stewed in red wine with bacon pieces, mushrooms and baby
onions. Trays of potatoes, bowls of crisp, green salad carefully tossed in a
dressing of mild mustard, lemon juice and walnut oil. Slabs of cheese and
a selection of fruit that would have shamed the harvest festival display in
any half-way decent cathedral.

Now to make *coq au vin* for thirty-odd hungry people who have
been stooping in low vines and reaching high with heavy baskets of grapes
and who love their food so much that a wine grower foolish enough to
skimp on the quality of his meals could quickly find himself with no help,

is a difficult enough task under ideal conditions, with plenty of time. Ideally you would start jointing your chickens and browning them in bacon fat at about six in the morning, so that you could simmer the large pots slowly through the forenoon while, with the help of two or three deft-fingered assistants you prepare the *crudités* and salads, chatting merrily and slurping wine, to produce this banquet with panache at twelve o'clock precisely.

But, you see, because the film crew would have to be paid overtime if they started before the agreed contractual hour we couldn't start at 6 a.m. In fact, as it turned out, owing to insignificant hiccups like the plugs on the leads not fitting the French sockets, I was not able to start until about 10.15 a.m. And, of course, I was not allowed to have an assistant, although I must admit that Andy, the assistant cameraman, himself no mean gastronaut, took pity on me and scraped and peeled and washed vegetables and salads for all he was worth.

You see it was not even a restaurant kitchen, it was a domestic kitchen, with just four electric rings and a small oven. Not at all suitable for such a gargantuan repast. (Note, I don't want to be a whingeing complainer and I don't want you to think that this is sour grapes, but unlike some TV programmes, we don't have the benefit of a brigade of trained home economists, cleaners and washers-up to help us.)

Anyway, the thing got underway and time was running out. I was on a hiding to nothing: if lunch was not ready by noon, such credibility as I had established with Madame and Monsieur Le Clerc was out the window, his workforce would be down the road and the BBC team might just have to give up filming for a few days and spend two or three back-breaking weeks picking grapes. Pritchard, of course, thought all of this was wonderful. With a childlike innocence that seemed, to me to have Machiavellian undertones, he beamed and directed away like directors do, cheerfully saying, '*Don't worry Floydy, you can do it,*' and under his breath, '*If you can't, you're fired.*'

I was taking every short cut I knew. I had the wine all ready in a saucepan, bubbling away to burn off the excess alcohol before adding it to the chicken. Suddenly Pritchard's good humour had gone, and he wanted to know why I was standing there doing nothing. I said, 'It's very simple, sunshine, the lids must go on the pots and the chicken must simmer until it is cooked. Only then, in about one hour's time, can you have the shots you want of the completed dish.'

If you can't do it, you're fired

'*That doesn't matter,*' he said. '*What I want now is to see the grape-pickers trooping in from the fields, whistling and singing in happy anticipation of their lunch. So go over the road and tell the farmer I want them here now.*'

'I can't,' I replied. 'They're not finishing work until 12 noon, then they come in.' We argued for five minutes and he reluctantly agreed to wait until the proper time.

It was then that the blow fell. As Bertie Wooster would say, 'There we are, up and smiling, the sun is shining and everything is going well, when fate slaps you round the back of the neck with a wet cod . . .' It was at this moment that the oven blew up, the bubbling stopped, and the television lights went out. I panicked, Pritchard waved frantically at me, the cameraman changed his lens for the reduced light and we carried on filming in the dark. Fine, good television, but the lunch had turned to rat. Madame Le Clerc came to the rescue. Burning our fingers we carried the hot pots across the busy road to neighbouring houses and without saying 'please' or 'thank you' we stormed in and commandeered their cookers, their gas rings and their ovens to complete the cooking.

There was a happy ending, the *coq au vin* was cooked and pickers came in from the fields. They had their lunch, they cheered, they clapped and they stayed to pick the grapes of Gevrais Chambertin.

AS IF THIS WASN'T ENOUGH, THE NEXT DAY THEY'D ARRANGED for me to borrow a little corner of a kitchen in the Hotel de la Cloche in Dijon, one of the most prestigious hotels in France, with at least two, three or five stars in the *Michelin Guide* and a very famous head chef. Well, the idea was I would take a corner of the kitchen, and prepare a simple peasant dish typical of the region. I, in fact, chose to cook some boiled ham in a piquant cream sauce, very simple.

The only thing was that about four hours before we were going to start they changed their plans and invited all of the chefs from all the good restaurants of the region to sample my cooking, which was really great. Because I had to go and do the shopping and then soak the ham in the bath in my room in the hotel overnight to get it ready, and then I had to cook for eighteen of France's top chefs. The only trouble was they had told the chefs to be there at five o'clock, but they said to *me* I didn't have to have the meal ready until six. So half-way through David said, '*Never mind whether it's cooked or not, serve the damn thing, because they've all got to go to work.*'

Anyway, I managed it and they gave me a golden hat for my trouble.

The good thing about being in France was that I escaped, for the time being at least, the personal appearances thing. In the privacy of our little crew I can act, overact, perform, let myself go without difficulty. Their professionalism and support makes that easy. But facing live audiences makes me weak at the knees and, worse still, makes me feel an utter fraud.

The bad thing about being in France was the little hiccups we had, like never having any maps, David always getting up late in the morning, going to restaurants for lunch when they were shut – if we even had time for lunch – and there never seemed to be any hotel rooms. God knows how they get those BBC wildlife teams up the Amazon.

We had really useful people coming to help us translate, I didn't need any translation, but everybody else did and I didn't see why I should have to do all the translation all of the time. The best and the most

God knows how they get those BBC Wildlife teams up the Amazon

Just as we were about to start filming 'Floyd on France' Floyd and I fell out very, very badly indeed. We fell out because Keith said to me that the only reason we were in France was because of him and his selling of the books; it was nothing to do with the TV programmes, just the fact that he could sell books that created the money that allowed the film to take place. I tried to explain that without the filming he would still be a semi-bankrupt restaurateur frying chips in Bristol, and that didn't go down terribly well.

I walked off into the night and went to my hotel room. The next morning when my assistant brought my mail from England I told her I didn't think there would be a French series at all, I couldn't work with this wanker. I asked her to work out how much it would cost to cancel such an elaborate series, which had already been started.

But as I opened my mail, strangely enough there was a letter written by me, to me. It was a letter I'd written when I was on

unlikely was darling Debbie Donlin, a Russian-speaking vegetarian, who was a great support when things got a little tricky, shall I say. And there were many other little niggles. You know, getting the rushes back, returning the cars we'd borrowed, saying thank you to the people whose houses we had just trampled over.

It all came to a head on that lovely Provençal evening as we were sitting on the sidewalk under the plane trees, the smoke rising up from the charcoal grill, eating kebabs, drinking iced rosé and Pastis. David and I had the most monumental row which almost stopped the entire shoot. It was absolutely appalling, I could have put an axe through his head, I really could. But because I am an amazingly fair person, I don't think it's right for me to comment on any of this, so here is an account of the argument in David Pritchard's own words.

one of these BBC management courses in which I had had to list all my worst faults. They'd told me it would be sent to me at some future date. It happened to be this day. Very humbly I phoned Floyd to discuss our differences.

DAVID PRITCHARD

Nearly right, David!

If you think I'm being contradictory then I'm sorry. Working in TV is full of contradictions. No matter how frustrated I became with Pritchard and his way of working, he is undisputedly a superb director, and if you subscribe to the view that it's the result that counts, he certainly comes up with the goods. And I know for a fact, though they've never told me, that when things are going badly for me during filming and I can't get it right, either Clive or Andy will fabricate some temporary technical fault to delay things a bit so I can get my act together.

CHAPTER 15

ON THE ROAD AGAIN

A Cri de Coeur for no more: Dinner Parties, Courgettes, After Dinner Speeches, or Cocktails with Mandarins.

I RETURNED FROM THE FIRST SHOOT IN FRANCE EXHAUSTED, but that awfully nice chap who manages my affairs had organized a few outings for me.

The first time I met John Miles I was in fact working for the BBC as a location caterer and I also ran a dial-a-dinner service to take food to people's homes. It used to be a bit disappointing sometimes delivering *coq au vin*, pheasant and jugged hare to a prefab estate, only to find that it had been a hoax call. Anyway, on the sayso of a BBC producer, I decided I

Tel. Bristol 33786
37799

A new Home Gourmet Service bringing the finest traditional English Home Cooking and French Haute Cuisine — direct to your dining room

FLOYD'S FEASTS

First class food without fuss or preparation — all you do is choose your menu and phone BRISTOL 33786 and a really superb meal will be delivered direct to your door!

If you like good food but you can't spend all day cooking, you'll find this new Home Gourmet Service a real boon. Whether it's a few friends, the boss and his wife, or a big family celebration, you can depend on FLOYD'S FEASTS to take care of the food while you take care of the guests......It's like having your own personal chef in the kitchen!

Here's how the service operates:
You choose your menu—you can if you wish choose a different meal for each guest, just as in a restaurant. Then you phone in your order—we are open from 10 a.m. to 12.0 p.m. seven days a week. Please try to give us your order at the very latest before 7 p.m. on the day the food is required.

If you prefer to heat and serve the menu of your choice in your own dishes, we can supply the food ready-cooked and deep-frozen for you to keep until needed in your own fridge. All the items shown on the menu opposite are guaranteed to keep fresh in the frozen food compartment of a domestic fridge for up to 30 days. Full instructions for defreezing and heating each dish are included with the special tinfoil containers. The DeepFreeze Service means you can always have a first class meal ready in case of emergencies or unexpected guests...(even a husband can follow the instructions!)

You may if you wish order just the main course, either piping hot or deep-frozen, so that you can serve your own hors d'oeuvres and sweets.

EXECUTIVE LUNCHEONS—Executives with a lunchtime conference on hand can arrange with Floyd's Feasts to have meals of their choice delivered to the Boardroom within minutes of telephoning.

MINIMUM ORDER   Two main courses
MAXIMUM ORDER   Forty complete meals

The Chef-Maitre
Keith Floyd has been an accomplished chef and restaurateur for six years, specialising in traditional English cooking and French haute cuisine. An ex-lieutenant in the Royal Armoured Corps, he is one of the few Englishmen totally dedicated to providing really superb food.

MENU

hors d'œuvres

Fresh Fruit Juice
Chef's Paté
Fish Soup
Borscht
Potage St. Germain
Iced Cucumber Soup
Minestrone Soup
Soupe du Jour

Courgettes Provençale (cold)
Taramasalata (cold)
Smoked Salmon Mousse (cold)
Potted Trout (cold)
Prawn Cocktail (cold)
Smoked Buckling (cold)
Chicken Vol-au-Vent (hot)

main courses

Hungarian Goulash
Steak, Kidney & Oyster Pie
Game Pie
Herring à la Moutarde
Spaghetti Bolognaise
Kidneys in Red Wine
Braised Tongue in Madeira Sauce

Dover Sole Mornay
Coq au Vin
Poulet Chasseur
Pork & Black Cherries
Poulet à la Kiev

Canard à l'Orange
Poached Salmon & Hollandaise Sauce
Fillet Steak with Huntsman Sauce—on croûte with paté

puddings

Sherry Trifle
Home-made Ice Cream
Sorbet—various flavours
Famous Liqueur Fool
Fresh Fruit Salad
Apple Pie and Cream

+ 10% service and delivery charge.

ALL MAIN COURSES include
vegetables, salad, potatoes or
rice (SORRY NO CHIPS!)
and garnishings the chef thinks
necessary.

needed a brand new van to cope with a filming job I was going to have to cater for, and he, of course, promised to pay me upfront – or certainly a good advance – so I gaily went along to have the roof of my van extended and certain bodyworks rearranged so I could use it as a mobile kitchen. And would you believe, the person who owned the garage (as a sideline) was John Miles, who came to be my manager. So I went to collect the van and said, 'Is it ready?'

He said '*Yes*'.

I said, 'Good, can I drive it away?'

He said, '*Not until you have paid*'.

I said, 'But I'll pay you in a couple of weeks just as soon as the BBC send me their cheque.' (This all sounds very familiar to me.) I was absolutely desperate, I mean I needed the van that afternoon to load in the generator and the microwave oven and gas cookers and stuff like that, and I was filming tomorrow, but he was absolutely adamant, no money, no honey.

I went away utterly dejected, went round to all my friends and scraped the money together and took it back at about ten to seven, just before he was shutting. He counted out every last penny of it before he released it to me and I drove it away cursing him, I really did. Of course, now that he, in a sense, is working for me, he applies the same attitude to the BBC, to ad agencies and to people who employ me and thank God for that.

SO HE ARRANGED ALL THESE LITTLE TASKS FOR ME. OPEN A kitchen shop in Barnstaple, give a cookery demonstration in Aberystwyth, a very quick photo session, a reception at Claridge's, a quick down the line chat for 'Woman's Hour', a short appearance on 'Jim'll Fix It', compère a catering exhibition in Darlington, pop back to London to record a voice over for a commercial, have lunch with someone from Saatchi and Saatchi, give a quick ten-minute chat on the phone for a live radio show, draw the raffle at the rugby club ladies' night in Bristol. Not to mention sampling wine for a wine society, writing my column for the *Sunday Express*, writing *Floyd on France*, making an appeal for Children in Need in Plymouth, presenting 'Down Your Way' from Dorset, speaking at the wardroom of HMS *Raleigh* after dinner in Plymouth, doing a live

Keith Floyd, David Pritchard and David Grant (Chairman of Glenfiddich)
May 1987

Recording 'Down Your Way', 1987

'Woman's Hour' in Devon and being hounded by the press who want details of my divorce – and flying to Scotland to collect the Glenfiddich Award.

Then, to make me feel better, he reels off a similar list of engagements he's had to turn down because there is no time to do them. And everybody, but everybody, wants you to decide now and do it tomorrow. As with a TV commercial, you spend months discussing the script, the price, the dates, the clothes you must wear, then a silence for, say, two or three weeks. Then a call. Sorry, we've got to do it tomorrow.

For one of these ads it was going fine, but I kept stumbling over the words: 'It's a vision'. Time and again the director, or if he was happy, the client, or if he was happy, the agency, or if they were happy, the continuity lady, was unhappy about my inflection. I repeated it so many times that it lost all meaning. Finally the director said, *'Listen love, have a little restette in your caravan and then we'll crack it.'*

It's at this moment you would despair, but for the wag from the crew, and there is always one. This time he took me to one side and told me of the day a very, very important actor had to leap from some French windows and utter one word, 'outrageous'. All morning this famous person, hand clapped to his head, was wandering around rehearsing in various theatrical tones the word 'outrageous' – presumably driving everyone around him mad. Time came for the take. They went to twenty-four till he too was asked to go to his caravan for a little restette. After a suitable time the director enquired if he was OK. Yes. Super. No probs.

Absolutely ready. They turned over, he flung open the French windows, leapt perfectly on to his marks and in ringing, magnificent tones delivered the line, 'Astounding'.

THE ADVERT THAT REALLY AMUSED ME, THOUGH, WAS ONE I did with the frogs. We had the most wonderful set – a Provençal kitchen – a funny script and a brisk director – by the way, there are so many people on a commercial set, it takes most of the morning to work out who the director is – the whole nine yards. They treated me really well, packets of Marlboro ready, endless coffee, a car back to Bristol, first-class hotel and a super fee which was rather more, in fact a lot more, than the dear old BBC had paid me for *three* series of 'Floyd On'.

The frogs had their own minder, plus a vet, plus a trainer. I might have to take and retake under hot lights for an hour or two at a time. Not the frogs. After each leap from the saucepan, which they did with careful supervision and thoughtful persuasion (honestly), they had to have a rest in their portable pond, and be checked by the vet. That's if they could be found, of course. Because no one could control their leap path, and they shot out like scalded cats from a sack, every which way, much to the delight of that happy band of chaps who on a commerical seem to spend the best part of the day sleeping under copies of the *Sun*, in various quiet but comfortable corners of the studio.

THE NEXT DAY JUDITH (MY PERSONAL ASSISTANT) AND I SET off for Aberystwyth where that night I had to give a cookery demonstration for the Electricity Board, and open their catering fair the next day.

Though why they employed me again after the disaster in Chester I'll never know. Christ, I could have died. In fact I think I did. It was, as they say, like this:

Joan Dittrich from the Manchester Electricity Board asked me to pop up to do a quick demonstration for a few of their employees. She's nice, the money was good, so 'right', I said, 'OK'. Now I'd done a couple of things like this before. In Barnstaple I opened a Schreiber kitchen shop. It's great, you roll up, they give you lots of drink, take you out to lunch and by then a large crowd has gathered to meet you, perhaps to get an autograph or a photo. Then I am surrounded by cheerful people who've come quite voluntarily and for free to see me, and I cook a couple of simple dishes, have a few slurps, tell a few jokes about Clive or Richard – the public are fascinated by both of the cameramen on our show – dish out a few samples, pose for local press photos and everyone's jolly happy. They all tell me I'm thinner/fatter/younger/older/more handsome/uglier than I am on TV. Everybody is very happy, I get a nice cheque and Judith drives me home. Terrific.

Imagine my feeling when I arrived at the address Joan had given me in Chester and found it to be the headquarters of Manweb, where they were holding their annual seminar. Training sessions, film shows, special lunch, I mean like an annual conference, and they'd booked me as the star turn in the bloody theatre for Christ's sakes! And the audience was the Electricity Board's home economists who were not about to be easily fooled by a fast-talking TV chef, whom most of them hadn't heard of anyway. And I was supposed to perform for them for two hours! I had no 'show' or 'plan', and I was petrified at the thought of facing so many people.

They had a video screen, the lot. And the latest halogen hob electric cookers that I couldn't understand. And, unbelievably, the only saucepans they could get had battered and rounded bottoms that barely touched the space-age heat emanating from the glass hobs.

I made all the jokes I could and got on with the 'show'. Everything depended on me producing a series of dishes that rolled off the stove one after the other without long or awkward pauses or gaps for me to fill. But I hadn't reckoned on the genius of the Electricity Board. Of the three stoves only one and a half of them worked at any one time. Quite simply if I turned on all the rings the fuses blew. But worse, it wasn't until I removed two very important dishes from the ovens with a flourish,

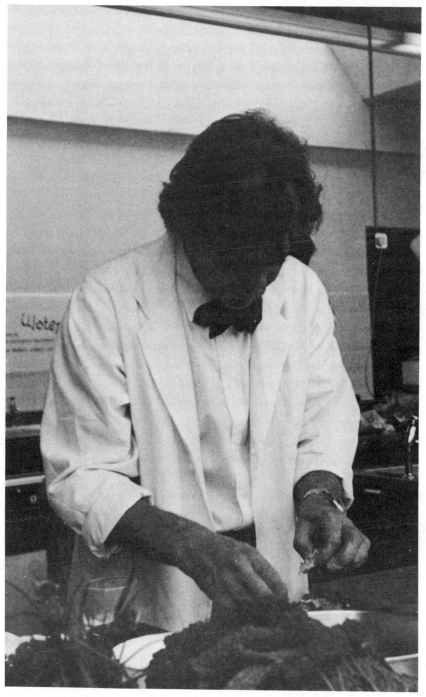

I don't usually cook in front of human beings

completely raw and uncooked, that I realized I hadn't switched the bloody things on.

I was devastated and dried up. I could think of nothing whatsoever to say. The audience that I couldn't see in the dark started talking amongst themselves. Some started to leave. My attempts to tell my Sherlock Holmes' joke, you know the one which ends, 'Because I was with you, you idiot,' had to be aborted when I suddenly remembered the vast majority of the audience were ladies . . . The local press had turned up in force — they loved it and, in fact, once I admitted defeat and jumped off the stage and started talking on a more direct basis with what was left of the audience, I managed to salvage the last twenty minutes.

I must say the Electricity Board people were better actors than I. Over a superb dinner that night at the Chester Grosvenor (a great place to stay by the way) they told me repeatedly that I was marvellous and everyone had loved it. Especially when I blew up the cookers.

After the Aberystwyth demonstration held in the university theatre, which was a success this time, we had the usual round of drinks and extravagant meals and hit the road back to London for another TV commercial, and, do you know, for the life of me I can't remember what the product was. Never mind. We filled the next two weeks before filming started again by hurtling around the British Isles, researching food and recipes for the next book and series, 'Floyd on Britain and Ireland'. This started as a cheerful gastronomic odyssey, and ended in a Rennie-chewing nightmare.

Basically everybody — every chef, every hotel — was so generous and hospitable that our stomachs really couldn't take it. I remember that towards the end we always parked the car as near as possible to the front door of the hotel, and took only an overnight bag in so we could escape early in the morning to avoid a mighty breakfast and more champagne. I've been off champagne every since that trip. (Though Pritchard still owes me a bottle from a couple of years ago when we were filming 'Floyd on Food' — which he 'inadvertently' drank one afternoon in his office.)

IF YOU HAD PASSED ME ON THE MOTORWAY DURING THAT time you'd have thought what a posing little shit I was. Me, middle-aged and wearing sunglasses, car phone in hand, swishing up the highways and byways in a drop-dead Jaguar with a blonde driving. But honestly, I was so busy: I had to check scripts, do newspaper interviews, argue with Frances or Pritchard about times and money as we sped on to the next gargantuan feast. Tell you what, if you need a real rest take a few days at the Isle of Eriska, or at Lady Veronica's place in Strachur and hang a few on with Jimmy McNab. NB. Beware of the McPhunn!

Where have the good old real Italian restaurants gone, by the way? You know, the *trattorie* where they had tuna salads and proper pasta, cheap, cheerful with singing waiters who load you with espresso coffee and Strega and Amarettos and not a pizza in sight? It deserves some looking into, does that.

Of course you get interrupted eating these wonderful meals by fans of the programme wanting to know what I'm drinking, or if they can have an autograph. I love it and welcome them, but the best kick I get is the looks on the faces of people who've never heard of me or seen me, wondering why the hell that guy is getting such wonderful attention. They look quizzically at you. Then whisper about you. Finally they ask the waiter, and what's so funny is that they're none the wiser when they're told.

People talking about you can be unnerving though. On one occasion I was eating a simple but delicious spaghetti bolognaise.

Nearby two elderly gentleman, clearly widowers, retired generals or captains of industry, were having, it seemed to me, their regular fortnightly lunch together. I'm not a curious person, and paid no attention to their conversation till I heard them talking about food. And television programmes. To make this dialogue authentic you must insert lots of 'ers' and 'umphs', and a really plummy accent.

'What was that fellow called, Australian wasn't he?'

'Yes. You mean Graham Carr. The, er, Galloping Gourmet.'

'That's the fellow. Super.'

'Yes, I suppose, but I like that bearded fellow on 'Food and Wine'. Crafty Cook they call him.'

'*The gal who does the wine is very knowledgeable, too.*'
'*Yes, much better than Janet Robertson.*'
'*Course it all started with David Harven, didn't it?*'
'*Don't remember him. Fanny Haddock was my favourite. The way she lashed into poor old Johnny.*'
'*Did you see 'Take Six Chefs?' That was quite brilliant. Especially that fella from Weston-Super-Mare. Cooks for Peter Caine the actor in London. What's his name. Sheppard. Something Sheppard.*'
'*Yes, but have you seen that fellow Floyd?*'
'*He's local isn't he? Yes, he lives in Taunton.*'
'*Bumptious fellow. Can't stand him.*'
'*Yes, he's a bit of an entrepreneur, awful.*'

As I left the restaurant I could not resist stopping at their table to say 'The good thing about TV is that you can switch it off', but as I paused to say so they looked up and in unison said,

'*My God, the man himself! We were just saying how much we enjoyed your programmes.*'

'*I wonder if you'd mind awfully signing this. It's for my grandson. He's such a fan of yours.*'

'Delighted,' I said.

DINNER INVITATIONS I DREAD. I RUN THE RISK OF BEING THE guinea pig for grotesque gastronomic experiments involving melting multi-coloured mousses, raw slivers of flesh daubed with banana purée and wedges of uncooked courgettes. All the result of a frantic, but misunderstood, research into some French culinary wizard's latest, very expensive, cookery book.

WHEN I WAS A BOY IN SOMERSET, THE OCCASIONAL ROAST chicken stuffed with parsley and thyme from the garden and served with a sauce (I suppose we called it gravy then) made from the giblets and feet of the freshly slaughtered bird was gastronomically exciting and theatrically hysterical. My grandfather would be ordered by gran to despatch a chosen bird which, of course, had first to be caught and as he had a tin leg . . .

NO SUCH LUCK THESE DAYS. PEOPLE ARE GENEROUS AND extravagant, but they often try too hard to impress by copying something they've once eaten at some amazing restaurant. If they stuck to something simple it would cost half as much and be twice as good.

One of the little tricks I have learned to avoid eating the vast quantities of food that people put in front of me is to respond over-enthusiastically to a question and ramble on into some long and boring story about my little experiences and get so involved in it that I let my food get cold and in the end they just take the plate away.

Why don't people pay more attention to the fundamentals of cooking, like fresh ingredients, carefully chosen and simply cooked? I wish they'd cook simple menus where the dishes complement each other in a balanced way, instead of the nausea-inducing flights of fancy that pass for modern cooking – which can, by the way, be fine when executed by a master.

Oh for a dinner of grilled goats' cheese with a bitter salad of *frisée* and radicchio tossed in walnut oil and lemon juice, followed by a free-range corn-fed chicken, roasted golden in butter, and served with its own juices along with matchstick chips and crisp, dark-green undressed watercress; and to finish, slices of British cooking apples sautéed in butter, flavoured with sugar and lemon juice, flamed in Calvados and served with thick, yellow, crusty, clotted cream.

ON ONE OCCASION TO GET OUT OF EATING MY COURGETTES
and avocado I told them about the day I was invited to have drinks with
the Director General of the BBC – Michael Checkland. I was terribly
excited – it's a bit like being invited to Buckingham Palace, a great
honour.

And my dear manager promised to keep the rest of the day clear
of appointments so I could go up to London relaxed and refreshed and
enjoy the party, which incidentally was attended by such notables as
Derek Jameson and Terry Wogan and one of the Drs Who. To be honest,
they were the only three people I recognized – the others were so famous I
couldn't place their names. The trouble is that when I get into a room full
of BBC executives (as David Pritchard will only too happily testify) a
strange personality change occurs in me and I find myself telling the
wrong people the wrong things. Like my long erudite and passionate
speech about true British cooking.

I was explaining things like tripe, black pudding and the joys of
offal – all those sort of things – in graphic detail to quite a big man with
glasses who, now I look back on it, seems to have had a sort of chilly aura
around him, as if he was one of those invaders from outer space who have
only adopted a human form for the purposes of their satanic intentions to
take over the earth. He stood there for a long time listening to me; he
neither twitched nor moved, his eyes were glassy and still and he had a
pleasant enough smile on his face, but eventually he excused himself to
talk to another guest. It was not until I picked up *The Sunday Times* that
weekend that I realized when I saw the man's face as large as life on the
centrefold, and that as a teetotal, non-smoking, vegetarian Buddhist, John
Birt, the Deputy Director-General of the BBC, probably had not really
appreciated my enthusiasm.

AS I WAS SAYING, HOWEVER, JOHN MILES, CHARMING AND
calm as ever on the morning I was due to leave to attend this party, said,
*'Oh, since we're up in London and there are only a couple of quick things
we could pop round to the offices of Pickwick and just sign the contract for
the tapes you are making. It won't take a minute.'* In fact it took four
hours – involving a tour of the factory and a full scale creative brain-

storming session with the producers, directors et al. Then, by way of relaxation we had lunch with Collins, jolly good it was too, high up in their smart building where we talked complex plans and deals for another book I was writing called *A Feast of Floyd*. To make matters even worse, some months ago I had accepted an invitation to speak that very night at the annual dinner of the West of England Booksellers' Association. But when the invitation from the Director General came, it was obvious that I could not turn that down and there was no way I could let the booksellers down. Apart from it being unprofessional, they really do earn me my money by selling my books. I was on the horns of a dilemma.

We finished lunch at four o'clock. Publishers' lunches are not noted for being teetotal, so it was with a very heavy head that I proceeded to Broadcasting House at six o'clock and committed a series of *faux pas* – the one I have already mentioned, and another one when Derek and Terry – my new chums – were enthusiastically listening to my tales of bitter complaint about the dear old BBC. I, of course, failed to read the signs in Terry's eyes and had not noticed the fourth person who had joined us, till Terry finally said, '*Keith, I don't think you've met Jonathan Powell have you?*'

'No,' I cried cheerfully, 'I don't believe I have. How do you do, and what do you do?' I said.

Terry in that deadpan way he has said, '*Jonathan is the Controller of BBC1, Keith.*'

It was at that moment that John Miles rushed up, fearing that I was going to put my foot even deeper into it, and dragged me outside to a waiting car to rush me to Paddington. He was not very friendly on the train, he clearly thought I had overstepped the mark and spent the journey looking at me in a marked manner. The train got to Bristol, I jumped into another waiting car and was driven at breakneck speed to the hotel in Exeter and arrived shattered to a great round of applause just as they were finishing their coffee. I had made it.

The booksellers were most concerned about my welfare, saying, have a drink, have a sandwich and relax before you go and speak – they had been waiting patiently for two hours for me to turn up. I, optimistic fool that I am, said, 'No, no, let me do it, I'm ready right now.'

The applause died away, I stood up and tried to put together a speech. But I was just too tired. I bottled out, explained that I had had a busy day and was not really up to making speeches. I felt dreadful. And the next morning, for God's sake, it was up with the lark hurtling to Newcastle to cook a barbecue for a kids' TV series. Why do I do it I ask myself?

CHAPTER 16

BE MY GUEST

On joining the Jet Set. Well nearly. And in praise of Real Cooks.

THE LITTLE PLANE SWOOPED AND DIPPED LIKE A CROW, playing with the turbulence over a cornfield. It was a bright November morning with a blue sky and freshly laundered clouds. Just when I thought the journey was nearly over our hosts distributed champagne and smoked salmon. I don't like champagne at the best of times – and at 9.30 in the morning, balancing like a kid on a roundabout, cold and cramped, I liked it even less. And I realized that we still had some time to go. The other guests, according to the list that they gave me in the PR handout, included Fay Maschler, a woman who by her frequent and sensible well-balanced attacks on the *Good Food Guide* in her *Evening Standard* column had often cheered me up when I was a restaurateur, feeling hurt, bitter or neglected by my latest entry in the *Guide*.

There were Fleet Street diarists, a man from *The Grocer* who chattered away spotting landmarks from the plane, and Albert Roux, who was, along with me (justified in his case, bizarre in mine), the guest of honour at the lunch to celebrate the 1987 vintage of Chablis at the Maison Laroche. And a handful of other assorted fun-loving journalists and PR people. It was, in the words of the old song, 'A long way to Tipa-drinkdown'.

We landed at a military airstrip and were driven to the *caves* for pre-luncheon drinkypoos. This was a beautiful building of dust-free stone walls, racks of bottles piled high, glinting in the soft electric light. We stood sipping our Chablis on the flagstones worn smooth by generations of wine-growers, pickers, merchants and imbibers.

Handsome men and elegant women (at least the French cont-ingent were) sipped and chattered as photo-flashes exploded and a man in trainers, a leather jacket and sunglasses (maybe the Truffaut of tomorrow) videoed the festivities. There is that smell, that atmosphere, style and *élan* that tells you, even if you had parachuted into the place blindfold, that you are in France. There is an understated simplicity about such proceedings that gives a paradoxical air of sophistication.

It was cold as we crunched up the neat gravel drive to the big house with its dovecote and clock tower. Under my warm, long British overcoat I felt at ease and at home for the first time in months.

A gaily decorated marquee had been erected and waiters in dinner jackets showed us to the tables. Outside, under the pale shadow of the clock tower, pink-faced apprentices in starched white watched over spits of plump yellow ducks roasting slowly over fires of vine roots. Although it was November, it reminded me of the hot evenings in Provence when the street cafés grilled *brochettes* and the air was heady with the aroma of Pastis, Gitanes and *herbes de Provence* and of when, to the amazement of the *citoyens* of L'Isle sur la Sorgue, I, an Englishman, opened the doors for the first time of a little restaurant.

They brought in the duck which was crispy golden on the outside and pink on the bone with a haunting flavour of the *feu de bois*. The wines were exceptional and the speeches flattering. They named the first pressing of this year's vintage *cuvée*, 'Albert Roux'.

He is a lovely man. Animated, dictatorial, a lover of offal and a smoker. He is able to create modern culinary masterpieces not because he subscribed to *A La Carte* for six months, but because he learnt at a very early age to chop the meat for an *andouillette*, to simmer a *plat côte* gently for a *pot au feu*, from friends and family who understood instinctively that ingredients for food, be they simple or exotic, must be fresh and treated with respect. He is the kind of man who, if at home had to polyfilla the walls or mix some cement for a garden wall, would add a bit of salt and pepper and an egg to the sand and cement.

What I am trying to say is that had he started life as a hod-carrier for a bricklayer, they would now be asking him to restore and replace the gargoyles on the west face of Wells Cathedral. There is no mystique about being brilliant if you really know what you are talking about.

People complain about him using his fingers, but there's nothing wrong with that – I use mine, but I have exceptionally clean fingers.

ALBERT ROUX

AS NIGHT FELL AT THE AIRPORT, ALBERT AND I LEFT THE rest of the gaggle shivering on the runway and very sensibly cheered ourselves up with a slight drinkette in the bar.

Airborne again they started pouring more champagne. I was feeling good and lunch had been fine, the cooks had worked well. The little plane was grinding through a head wind, but at least the pilot put the heating on! I dozed and as I nodded off a diary of events ran through my brain like a ticker-tape. I wish there was a way of writing a book by going to bed, fixing electrodes to your head and waking up to find it printed out the next morning.

CHAPTER 17

SING FOR YOUR SUPPER

Which demonstrates the Serious Side of Floyd's Culinary Skills and explains the essential Difference between Himself and a Jog.

BY NOW I'D GOT USED TO OPENING KITCHEN STORES AND supermarkets and stuff like that. What I hadn't planned for was that people started asking me to do cookery demonstrations in theatres. Well of course you can't go into a theatre and do a real cookery demonstration because, first of all, the audience can't see and anyway, I don't know how to do it, and somehow I felt obliged to give them some kind of entertainment. So I found a way of doing it which has been described by Michael Bateman, my esteemed, beloved editor on *The Sunday Express* magazine, as 'a combination of Dave Allan, Dame Edna, and Keith Floyd'.

So there I was, in places like Exeter, Chichester and Barnstable, on stage in front of sometimes up to 500 people. Well it was absolutely terrifying for me, if they'd actually paid money to come in and see me for some good cause like a festival, or charity, or something I felt even worse. I liked it best of all when I was doing it on an impromptu basis and for free. But with the help of Noola, the home economist, who once threatened to strip – I wish she had, it would have cheered things up – and Peter Bush who played the piano, and the OK Chorale who sang, we kind of shambled through . . .

SCENE: *Chichester Festival, July '87, in front of an audience of four or five hundred people.*

PETER BUSH: Ladies and gentlemen, I am proud to introduce the only graduate from the clingfilm school of catering, Floyd.

PART I

Stage is set with piano on left, working stainless-steel tables, three in 'L' shape and one cooker. FLOYD enters stage right, wearing blue trilby, white jacket, blue bow tie, blue trousers and clogs. Holding red briefcase.

FLOYD: This is my box [*briefcase*]. I don't usually cook in front of human beings! Normally it is only the television camera. [*Walks over to piano.*] I am actually terrified, so I apologize if the odd swear word should slip out. I don't know what I'm going to do yet, I might get drunk, but it's nice to be in Bournemouth! [*It's Chichester in fact.*]

This hat has nothing to do with my political beliefs, but I'm jolly pleased she got back in [*throws hat off stage*], and that's what I think of politics. What is going to happen is that Peter will play the odd song, and I must introduce you to my assistant, Noola. [*Noola walks on stage.*]

She has just come out of a drug clinic after years of heroin abuse, this is her first step on the road to becoming a proper person. The first trick she is going to perform is to light the two front gases and turn up the oven, otherwise we will be screwed.

This bottle of wine will be used like one of those Roman candles, i.e. to tell the time by. When this bottle is empty I am going home, whether the food is cooked or not.

[*Opens briefcase.*] Here I have a hip flask, my binoculars to see my mother at the back, some sweets, Rennies, a cucumber which we will be discussing later, a corkscrew, a clean hankie and a pen knife. [*Uncorks wine.*] The thing I don't like about theatres is that you are not allowed to smoke in them, but tonight, as I am the performer, I am allowed to as they have special things ready to put me out. [*Lights cigarette, Peter plays Hamlet cigar theme.*]

Tonight we are going to cook chicken in beer, langoustines in piquant tomato sauce, trout and then a pudding. [*Introduces OK Chorale who come on and sing.*]

I was petrified at the thought of facing so many real people

I learned how to make chicken in beer in Alsace in a town called Colmar. I
have jointed the chicken into tiny pieces and fried them in butter for
about half an hour. Next I season with salt and pepper and add some
finely chopped onion [*throws some into audience, Peter plays a song*].
Next chop some mushrooms and add to the chicken along with some
lemon juice.

It's frightening doing this you know. Last time in Exeter I was told off for
swearing, you get scared shitless. Now we will let that simmer.

Next we will make the tomato sauce. First blanch the tomatoes in boiling
water and peel, depip and chop. Fry some finely chopped onions in
olive oil with some peeled and crushed garlic, add the tomatoes and
reduce to a marmalade-like consistency, add some basil, parsley and
salt and pepper and a tablespoon of sugar and some white wine. Allow
to simmer for ten minutes. [*Peter plays a song, KF takes pans down to
audience to show.*] Next Noola liquidizes the sauce.

In Alsace they have home-made alcohols of prune, *quetsch* or raspberry,
but as we don't have that, we will use gin [*KF pours gin into pans, huge
flames, audience gasps*]. Next add some beer, turn up the gas and put
the lids on the pans. [*Peter plays a song.*] Yes, Peter, we will let you
know! He is actually my insurance broker, but begged me to let him
appear on the show.

We will next fry the langoustines for a few seconds in olive oil and add
some chopped onion and salt and pepper and shake the pan. Next add
some brandy and flame. We did ask the organizers to provide some
new, shiny stainless-steel pans! [*brings out old stained meat trays*].
While we cook the rest of the langoustines the OK Chorale will sing for
you.

Now the gas has failed on the cooker. [*Peter plays to order, transpires
that KF has in fact turned it off!*] We now pour our tomato sauce over
the langoustines, sprinkle with some tabasco or chilli sauce and
sprinkle with parsley.

[*Picks up cucumber in wrapper.*] The thing about cucumber sandwiches
is that they should be prepared with the utmost care. Pick one from
your cloche, sharpen your best knife. Take off the wrapper – it's funny
because most things nowadays have to be kept on! [*Chucks cucumber
away, sits down and lights cigarette, takes food down to the front and
thousands of people rush up to taste the fish.*]

Now we will recap on the chicken in beer. We are now left with an oily, grey liquid which we will strain into a saucepan. Bring to the boil and reduce by about one third. [*OK Chorale come on and sing Floyd song.*]

Add some double cream to the reduction and some knobs of butter. Pour the sauce over the chicken. [*Takes chicken to front of stage and announces five minutes' interval, and walks off stage.*]

PART II

FLOYD: [*OK Chorale open and Peter plays as KF re-enters through the curtain.*] Now we are going to cook the trout and we will cook it in newspaper. [*Picks up paper and starts to read.*] I was at school with Jeffrey! We like to choose the sort of newspaper our audience is familiar with, we have the *Telegraph* and *The Times* and a copy of the *Sun*. To cook a trout in newspaper we fill its insides with lemon slices, salt and pepper and parsley and then wrap the fish in two sheets of newspaper. Put into a bucket of water and squeeze tightly. Next we are going to make a hollandaise sauce. We don't need copper pans, only a food processor. Put six eggs in and whisk until frothy, squeeze in some lemon juice. [*Checks trout and has trouble closing oven door.*] Now we will melt the butter.

The pudding we are making is one of soft fruits with *crème anglaise*. To make this sauce properly you need half a dozen eggs and some castor sugar, etc., it takes hours. [*Picks up tin of custard.*]

Arrange the fruit in a dish, add some cream to the custard and whisk in some milk, spoon over the fruit.

Pour in the melted butter to the food processor. Pour out the hollandaise sauce and add some chopped fresh chives.

The other day I was whizzing up the motorway when I happened to overhear my name being mentioned on the radio so I tapped on the glass divide to alert my chauffeur to turn it up.

This person was saying, 'What's the difference between a jog and Keith Floyd?'

The answer was, 'One's a pant in the country . . .' and just at that moment we went under one of those motorway bridges and I missed the rest.

[*Peter sings a song.*]

We will now take out the trout [*cuts up newspaper and opens out trout –
shows to audience. Puts on to plate and pours sauce over, sprinkles
with parsley*].

Finally we sprinkle some sugar over the custard and put it under the grill.
[*OK Chorale sing some jingles, audience comes up to taste trout. Peter
plays a song and the OK Chorale come back on stage.*]

[*Serves pudding.*]

[*Exeunt.*]

CHAPTER 18

REFLECTIONS IN THE TORRENT

Flushed with the Success of scoring a Dramatic Try, our Hero wallows in Happy Nostalgia and even attempts a little Philosophy.

ONE OF THE MOST BRILLIANT INDIVIDUALISTIC TRIES SCORED in the history of Anglo-Welsh rugby will never, unfortunately, be included in Cliff Morgan's '100 Best Tries' video, or even on 'Rugby Special', which is a great loss to the thousands of rugby fans throughout the British Isles and, indeed, the world. I refer, of course, to the great occasion at Kidwelly Rugby Club, when I scored and converted the match-winning try.

I was playing out of position at fly half with Ray Gravell (Llanelli, Wales and British Lions), playing at scrum half. Naturally the pairing of Floyd and Gravell had a distinct psychological effect on our opponents, and they were a little jittery I'm sure. But my jinking side-step left their back row floundering after I took the long spinning pass from Gravell and I was left with a mere thirty-five yards to run to touch down under the post. In that true sportsmanlike manner, when I only had the full-back and the wing to beat, I gave Gravell a reverse-pass out of respect for his work in setting up the try. The two defendants, thinking they had a chance to stop the try, hit Gravell simultaneously, but they were not prepared for our scissors and I took back the ball and touched down unopposed.

It was the first try scored by an Englishman on that hallowed Welsh turf in the long history of the club. I was, of course, called upon to take the conversion. I composed myself, took my customary three and a half steps back and to the right and thumped the ball straight and true between the posts – thus securing an historic victory.

Happily the great occasion is not lost, because Richard Elliott filmed the whole thing for 'Floyd on Britain and Ireland'. I think it would be churlish of any viewer to notice that on the close-up of my boot pumping the ball over the post, the tanned muscled legs that kicked it didn't really appear to match my pale, spindly legs with their trim ankles. Neither would it be fair for any members of our film crew to reveal to the press that the whole sequence was completely set-up. But nonetheless it was a meritorious sporting achievement. It was a pity that either by design or accident – probably design – they decided that the first five takes of me scoring the try were unusable. In fact, I am certain that it was for their own private sense of fun that Pritchard said, barely able to hide his mirth, *'I am sorry, Floyd, could you just run that thirty-five yards flat out one more time, love?'*

It's also not easy running flat out down the pitch at the age of forty-three and wired for sound, explaining the finer points of cooking a cawl. One thing is very strange though. I did actually end up with a couple of fractured ribs and was in agony for several weeks. I mean, truthfully. I was running for my life with that suntanned bunch of Welsh hoodlums hot on my heels, who would quite happily have marmalized me.

By the way, in case you ever do want to make friends with a Welsh rugby club you need to know how to cook a cawl and at the very least you should know what it is and how to pronounce it (like cowl).

CAWL

1 tbsp lard or bacon fat
2 onions, coarsely chopped
4 carrots, coarsely sliced
2 parsnips, roughly chopped
1 swede, coarsely chopped
450g (1lb) piece of brisket of beef or neck of lamb (or both)
675-900g (1½-2lb) piece of smoked bacon (use collar or shoulder), soaked if necessary
12 black peppercorns
1 clove
1 bay leaf
sprig of fresh thyme
lamb or chicken stock – water at worst
450g (1lb) potatoes (preferably tiny and new)
4 leeks (slender and thin if possible)

Put the lard or bacon fat in a large soup pot and brown the onions, carrots, parsnips and swede. Remove and brown the meat in the fat. Return the vegetables to the pot with the meat and add the bacon and herbs. Cover with stock.

Bring to the boil, skim and simmer for 2–3 hours. If the potatoes are not new, cut into pieces. Add the potatoes 20 minutes before the end of cooking.

Meanwhile, finely chop the slender leeks. To serve, put a piece of meat in each bowl, along with broth and vegetables. Garnish with the finely chopped raw leeks. Serve together with a hunk of cheese and some bread.

THE GREAT THING ABOUT OUR PROGRAMMES IS THAT WE make them up as we go along and also, even though the films are obviously edited, I do cook in 'real time'. We don't have one already prepared in the oven. So it seemed quite logical that when I got to the stage of preparing the cawl and I have to say 'that now goes in the oven for two hours', I should then change into rugby strip and go and score a quick try.

It took me two hours to score that quick try and then trembling, bruised and battered I had to return to the club house, and dish up this cauldron of food to a hoard of ravenous rugby men. I was still wearing my strip but had replaced my boots with my usual clogs, much to the delight of the boys who called and whistled in very appreciative tones as I came tripping in with two bloody great serving plates piled high in either hand. Perhaps thinking I was still on the rugby field I attempted a side-step and a swerve past an obstructing table, and fell flat on my back causing the precious food to splatter across the club house floor. The boys, who had been singing some terrifying rugby song as I slid in, without missing a beat switched the tune to a primordial chant – the chorus of which I seem to remember was, 'silly billy, silly billy', repeated many, many times.

Luckily there was just enough left for everyone to have a taste and the afternoon proceeded in the waggish way that post-match celebrations do. You know, some tasteful singing, a bit of beer throwing, an exchange of the odd joke and the highlight of the whole occasion, nay the climax of a truly harmless boys' day out, was watching David Pritchard being set on fire.

He was so engrossed in explaining how his hand was having difficulty in making the glass meet his lips, that he didn't notice that he was on fire, but leapt like a scalded cat and rounded angrily on (unfortunately in my view) a really nice chap who poured a bucket of water over him to put him out! It was so funny that I completely forgave him for stitching me up the night before when he had told the organizers of a dinner given for the 'Friends of Oysters and Chablis Club', more impressively known as the 'Conferie de la mer' (merely another excuse to get pissed), that if he could film the opening ceremony of this somewhat secret circle of gastronauts I would be delighted to stay for the whole evening and give them an after-dinner speech. Of course, he forgot to mention this to me. So I found myself once again completely abandoned by the crew and my beloved director the second the filming was over.

'Hey, wait for me,' I said.

'Oh, you can't come, you have to stay and give them an after-dinner speech.'

'Thank you very much,' I said, 'Will it be OK for my agent to invoice you for my normal fee?'

'Oh, come on, don't be mean,' he said. *'You'll enjoy it.'*

'Great,' I said, 'Why don't you stay as well?'

'You must be joking,' he said. *'I don't want to spend an evening with a bunch of dickheads.'*

ANOTHER BRILLIANT PIECE OF FILMING WHICH I REALLY enjoyed was on the River Fyne in Argyll. The brief was as ever very simple and direct: *'Go and catch a salmon!'* Which, of course, to my director's annoyance (he fancies himself as an expert fisherman), I did. Naturally I was posing perfectly. Green wellies, tweed cap – the whole bit. I got very carried away and excited, but unfortunately David forgot to tell the cameraman to point the camera at the fish, so when we played back the video there was no fish to be seen. David was furious, and merely turned to me and said, *'Go and catch another one, and this time while you're doing it I want a fruity, philosophical and passionate piece to camera about the joys of salmon fishing.'*

Anyway we did catch another salmon. I got it on the line, Richard got it in the can and Lady McClean put it in the pot! And a merry time was had by all at the Creggans Hotel in Strachur, while Sir Fitzroy McClean, an arch story-teller if ever there was one, recounted the tale of his whisky – the dreaded McPhunn – that had, the night before, caused David across a crowded room to temporarily and harmlessly (by that I mean the object of his desire was not party to his feelings) fall in love with the barmaid. For a brief hour he radiated the sort of childish happiness that you are likely to see in a Peanuts or a Perishers cartoon.

The McPhunn had also taken its toll on an eighteen-stone local who had quietly fallen asleep, blocking the exit door; and in a foolish stint of heroism – actually a cunning attempt to impress the barmaid – David took courage in both hands, drank it and proceeded to remove the

He fancies himself as an expert fisherman

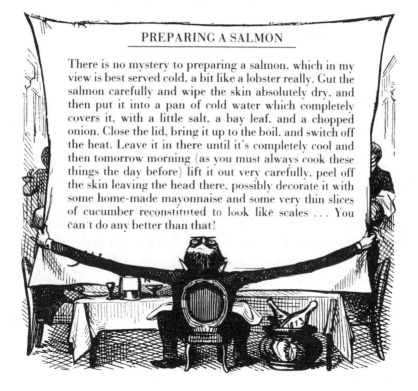

PREPARING A SALMON

There is no mystery to preparing a salmon, which in my view is best served cold, a bit like a lobster really. Gut the salmon carefully and wipe the skin absolutely dry, and then put it into a pan of cold water which completely covers it, with a little salt, a bay leaf, and a chopped onion. Close the lid, bring it up to the boil, and switch off the heat. Leave it in there until it's completely cool and then tomorrow morning (as you must always cook these things the day before) lift it out very carefully, peel off the skin leaving the head there, possibly decorate it with some home-made mayonnaise and some very thin slices of cucumber reconstituted to look like scales ... You can't do any better than that!

sleeping giant. For two or three brief but luxurious seconds, I re-wrote the scenario in my mind. Perhaps the sleeping monster would rear up from his drunken stupor and, like King Kong, balance David sweetly between his fingers and smilingly, with a huff and a puff, blow him into Loch Fyne. I must say, there is no way I would have attempted to shift the guy who, in fact, left happily, probably quite pleased that someone had taken the trouble to wake him up and tell him it was time to go home.

The last time we had attempted to catch a salmon was when we were filming on the River Exe. As luck would have it the water bailiff who knew everything about the river was already fishing and, of course, hooked a big one. The plan was that the moment he had a fish firmly on the line, he would hand it over to me and for television reasons I would get all the glory, although we would naturally confess a little bit later in the programme that it was a set up job. Trouble was I was still getting changed into my waist-high waders, etc., when the shouted instruction came, '*Quick, take the rod*,' but because I was dressed only in my red socks at the time I said, 'No, hang on I haven't got my boots on'. David said, '*It doesn't matter, it'll look very funny, you catching a salmon wearing your red socks.*' I refused to comply – the only time I have ever refused to do anything that David has asked me and actually I should have heeded his wishes. Result: a lost salmon, a disgruntled bailiff and a disapppointed me.

(That's enough fishing stories – ED.)

THAT'S THE TROUBLE WITH EDITORS, THEY KEEP LEAPING IN and telling you what to do. If I want to talk about fishing I am going to talk about fishing. Anybody who used to collect the *How to catch 'em* series, published by Herbert Jenkins, will understand what I am talking about.

Captain L. A. Parker's *Roach*, J. B. Walker's *Rods, How to tie artificial flies* by L. Vernon Bates, *The confessions of a carp fisher* by B. B., *Drop me a line* by Richard Walker. Even the names of the authors remind you of retired spies or characters from 'Dynasty', never mind what they wrote, like John Inglis Hall's *A love affair with a river*, a passionate tale. If, as I have said, you have been brought up on books like these then fishing means something to you.

When you are standing casting a fly you don't care any more

If, on the night before the opening of the coarse fishing season, you went to sleep tremulous with excitement and a piece of string tied to your toe dangled through your bedroom window, so that your mate could wake you with three tugs in the early dawn before you cycled through the mists to the Kings' Sedgemoor Drain with newly varnished rods and a box full of wriggling red worms and some carefully made bread dough to tempt a tench or a roach, you will know what I mean. These days, when I have a moment to steal time from myself and from television and stand alone in the burbling waters of the Black Water River in County Cork, I find a peace and a tranquillity, if not a fish, that releases the spool of my memory, and my thoughts and reflections alight upon the reservoir of my mind, like the flies landing on the stream.

You are free to say hello to the cow munching on the bank. You don't jump when a kingfisher darts by, like you do in your office when the phone rings. You remember things like the great franchise deal when they promised to buy your restaurant and launch you on a dazzling career. You remember every day that they phoned to say that the cheque was in the post; you remember every day believing it for nearly eight months. And although it caused you to bleed, when you are standing casting a fly you don't care any more. It really doesn't matter.

IN THE 1950s, WHEN A MAN CALLED HORSE DROVE THE DRAY for Arnold and Hancock's Brewery in Wiveliscombe, and the mornings were started by the siren, and on market days farmers in leggings and brown cotton overalls unloaded their cattle into the market, I first went fishing with my Dad.

Out of the town, past the rec. and before a sharp bend known as Devil's Elbow, there is a leafy lane that leads to a little reservoir. This triangular pond fed by a swift flowing stream from the Brendon Hills was where I caught my first fish. Dad made a rod from a raspberry cane and we used the waxed thread that my grandfather stitched shoes with as a line.

On that very special May morning over thirty years ago, we hid behind an elder tree and swung our bait into this mystical pool. The little crow's quill float − which, by the way, I had made myself − had barely settled in the water before it bobbed once and shot away. The fish took off with such force I don't think I even struck – it struck itself. Minutes or hours later, I'm not sure which, we landed this vibrant, flapping fish and wrapped it in dock leaves.

Today as I stand in the Black Water I think of Dad and that day and I think of the time that I was writing *Floyd on Fish*, and it's sad that he died before either the book was published or the films were transmitted. He would have been sad too, like me, had he returned to the Wiveliscombe reservoir.

The ornamental pond once owned by the Hancocks with its island of willows, bamboo and even arched bridge, forbidden to us village lads by the *droit de seigneur* and the iron fence that surrounded it, had silted up to merely a puddle, the bridge was rotten and broken, the reservoir had shrunk, the trees and bushes, the elder and alder had been cleared, leaving it naked. The magic was no longer there. I would like to catch a big fish today and take it back and put it on Dad's grave.

My Dad was a gentle and philosophical man. I wish he had lived – if only to see the sequence in 'Floyd on France' where Monsieur Pelican said, 'Give a man a fish and he will live for a day. Teach a man to fish and he will live forever.'

Dad would have liked that.

CHAPTER 19

THE MAGICAL MYSTERY TOUR

Floyd becomes an Expert on Train Timetables, chauffeur-driven Cars, and Sandwiches.

ACTUALLY WRITING AND PUBLISHING A BOOK LOOSELY BASED on a television series, as my cookery books are, should not be a problem. You merely block off a couple of months and settle down quietly to write.

The trouble is people like your manager and your director all think that it's such an easy process that they carry on booking you in for personal appearances or filming dates just the same, so you are always frantically chasing deadlines to get them finished. The worst bit, having written your book under desperate circumstances, and when you finally know that the television series *is* going to come out at the same time as the book, is the dreaded promotional tour.

Anyway, what follows now is a little diary that I shall call the *Anatomy of a Tour*.

1987
MONDAY 14 SEPTEMBER

Soft, sunny autumn day. Hood down on the XJS, bombing through the countryside for the first signing at 12.30 in Southampton. Give my bow tie a flick to make it look floppy, wash my hands, clean my fingernails and prepare to meet the waiting crowd. Shop manager says, *'Excuse me,'* and straightens my bow tie.

Successful signing, except that thirty or forty people are a bit disappointed because there are no hardbacks left.

You just block off a couple of months and settle down quietly to write

Into the back room for a glass of wine and a sandwich. It is 1.30 p.m. 1.45 – sitting in a radio station, answering questions from an interviewer who has not read my book, and has not seen the television programmes. 2.30 – same building, television studio, answering the same questions from a man who *has* read the book *and* seen the programme. I wish I had brought the rest of the sandwiches with me. Back into the car, hood down, bright sun to Salisbury. 4.30 – fight through a huge crowd, pose for pictures, sign books, drink the obligatory glass of red wine. Overnight in Bristol. Very satisfied.

TUESDAY 15 SEPTEMBER

Hood down, fine day, fast drive to Exeter, signing at 12.30. Slightly delayed by animal rights protesters who object to me eating meat, fish and fowl publicly on television. No sign outside the shop saying I am there, but a good turnout for all that. Lectured for twenty minutes by a man, who does not want to buy a book, about giving up smoking. Up in the stock room, another plate of sandwiches, from which I politely excuse myself and take my minder to lunch in a wine bar instead, before hurtling to Plymouth for a huge signing at 4.30 p.m. Quick radio interview with a chap who is *going* to read my book and will *try* to get a tape of one of the programmes.

The queue is silent and po-faced, until the manager of the shop puts a bottle of red wine and a glass on my signing table. A great cheer goes up and I sign books, photos and envelopes until 6.30. I then drive my minder back to Bristol at 140 mph the whole way and frighten the living shit out of her.

WEDNESDAY 16 SEPTEMBER

By train from Bristol to London, no restaurant or buffet car available, transfer to Didcot, just make the train to Oxford. Picked up at Oxford by the BBC rep to do radio interview. Desperate for coffee. 12.30 – interview finished, rush for the train to Birmingham, drop large hints about lunch and drink, arrive in Birmingham starving. Check into hotel, informal signing for an hour or two, no breakfast, no lunch, no sandwiches, nothing. Dinner at an Indian restaurant, much to the dismay of my secretary who hates Indian food.

THURSDAY 17 SEPTEMBER

8 a.m. train to Liverpool. Print interview, then signing at 12.30, can of lager and packet of crisps for lunch. Car to Manchester, 4 p.m. signing, videoed by a bunch of cowboys. Then to radio interview.

Desperate with hunger and unable to eat the extravagant and huge meal lovingly prepared by the people at Knutsford. During the Liverpool signing being interviewed by local radio, local paper, dozens of photo calls, smiling cheerfully all the time, have to laugh at the man who waited patiently in the queue for a book to be signed, because he thought I was a footballer, when he found out I was not said, '*Fuck this for a game of soldiers,*' and left.

The pattern was beginning to develop, that I am amazingly well appreciated by the public who give me presents of anything from home-made jam to scouse passports, or bottles of wine. But end up in the hotel at night starving, wrecked and unloved.

FRIDAY 18 SEPTEMBER

Owing to a serious fire missed the plane to London and arrive at the BBC Bush House bookshop without breakfast and no time for lunch. The one-hour's signing drags on for two and they seem annoyed with me when I leave for not having stayed long enough. Straight to a disorganized signing in Marylebone High Street. Home to Bristol.

SATURDAY 19 SEPTEMBER

Drive to Kingston-on-Thames for 11 a.m. signing before being driven to Bromley for a 2.30 p.m. signing and no lunch. Obligatory bottle of wine. Return to Bristol.

MONDAY 21 SEPTEMBER

Early train to London and then to Ipswich and two radio interviews before 12.30 signing. A gobbled lunch in the rain outside a charming little restaurant, where once again print interview and conned into publicity photos for somebody else's restaurant. Make the train to Norwich with seconds to spare, heartburn and indigestion. I don't think the minder has spoken to me for some hours. Arrive at Norwich. Time for a quick bath and then to a 7 p.m. talk and signing at a bookshop – again packed with Floyd fans. I tell them witty stories, sign their books, make them laugh. Back to the hotel and another plate of sandwiches.

TUESDAY 22 SEPTEMBER

At this point, as seemed to be happening with increasing regularity and frequency in my life those days, I exploded yet again. Things were not right. I needed a little bit more TLC, which, for those of you who haven't been to university, means tender loving care. And so, over a few late-night Tia Maria shandies, I had a few words with Laura who promised to sort things out.

Like a child on Christmas morning, fumbling for his stocking at the end of the bed, I open the curtains of my room to see if there is a neat chauffeur standing beside a limousine on the street outside – and there is. So we hop into the back of the big Volvo and a nice man in a peaked cap

drives us to Leeds. We even stop for breakfast on the way at a Little Chef, and have eggs and bacon and read the papers. It's very good to arrive in style at the bookshop at 12.30, met by the BBC rep and an enthusiatic crowd. After I have signed for one and a half hours, we go back in the stock room (I am becoming quite an expert on stock rooms) for, would you believe, another plate of sandwiches and the by now ubiquitous bottle of Gevrais Chambertin. In between mouthfuls answer questions from lady journalists. 3 p.m. – small reception at the BBC office, hosted by Harry Dunn – our man in the North – where we whack a few down feeling quite cheerful, while a man from the *Daily Mail* takes notes. This is the best ten minutes of the whole tour so far, but of course the schedule is tight and we must leave for Newcastle.

A slight hiccup occurs when I am told that the chauffeur-driven Volvo has to return to Norwich (boo hoo), but I cheer up considerably when a two-ton Roller pulls up on to the forecourt. I slip into the leather seats *en route* for Newcastle and the BBC television studio, for an interview with a man whose wife has read my book and whose auntie really likes the programme. A few drinkypoos with old friends before being taken to the hotel, which is a gothic castle. This trip is either a feast or a bloody famine.

One day I am dragging my suitcases down some provincial high street looking for some soul food and a place to eat and the next I am swooping up some manicured gravel drive in a Roller and sleeping in a four-poster bed in the King Charles Suite, that has a ceiling ninety feet high. A grotesque dinner, notwithstanding the grandeur of the surroundings, followed by a night's sleep interrupted by the ghosts next door being sick in the basin!

WEDNESDAY 23 SEPTEMBER

Dawn breaks and the dream has gone – like Cinderella's coach the Roller has turned into a 22-year-old stretched Ford Zodiac, dented with a rattly exhaust and no door handles. It's the sort of car that comes fifth in funeral processions. It's a long and winding road from Leeds to Newcastle at 35 mph. Arrive Newcastle 5.30 p.m. to a rapturous reception where I tell them what it's like going on an Author's Tour, slag off the BBC, sign about eight million books and get back in the old Ford starving and cold, watching the one broken windscreen wiper flap like a wounded crow over the dirty windscreen amidst the encircling gloom.

We arrive in Edinburgh about 10 p.m. and to my amazement the hotel, the Edinburgh Sheraton, turns out to be brilliant. I mean it's not exactly the Duke's Hotel, but the staff – like all Scots – are incredibly courteous and helpful. My room is great and there's a personal message of welcome from the manager, along with a bottle of champagne.

I am starving, but curiously terrified to go into the restaurant. The trouble is when I go to restaurants these days, particularly in chain hotels, the only meal likely not to make you throw up is a couple of grilled lamb chops – I mean three succulent cutlets from the carvery grilled to your liking on the charcoal grill and served with a freshly baked jacket potato and a selection of salads from the world from our serve-yourself salad bar. If I sit in the corner, facing the wall with my hat pulled down over my eyes and my nose buried in the newspaper I might just get it, but – once recognized – the awesome magnificence of their gastronomic menu, which normally involves cornets of smoked salmon stuffed with prawns, followed by *roulades* of fish and spinach and raw sculpted potatoes the size of marbles looking distinctly uncomfortable on a plate three foot square is rolled out before me.

The other thing that doesn't usually happen in such hotels is room service saying such things as, 'a succulent sliver of Scottish sirloin grilled to your liking, served on a freshly toasted baguette and served with fresh salad and french fries', and really titillating your palate after a hard day sitting in the back of a beaten-up Ford. But I press the telephone and order just that, along with horseradish, tomato ketchup and mustard (that generally means three more visits from the waiter), an ice-cream, a whisky, a pot of coffee, three bottles of Orangina and a Crunchie bar. To my amazement the whole lot comes whizzing up in five minutes – the steak is truly the best piece of steak I have ever had in my life outside of Ireland and everything is absolutely tickety-boo. All I have to do now is stay awake until 11.30 p.m. when I have to do a live telephone interview with some whacky radio station whose researcher told me that 'Big Ed, the presenter, is really looking forward to getting a copy of your book'.

The deal on these things is that they ring you five minutes before the programme starts and you hold the phone loosely, listening to the programme until it's time to go on. To kill the minutes waiting for the call I do as I always do, fill up my suitcase with every conceivable thing – bar of soap, shampoo, the goodnight chocolate and the plastic laundry bags in the bottom of the chest of drawers. I grab the phone off the hook as it rings and a lady's voice says, *'Hello, is that Keith Floyd?'* 'Yes.' *'Good,'* she says. *'There are a few of us downstairs in the bar who would like to meet you.'* I politely explain that she has to get off the line as I am waiting for an important call from a radio station; she won't take no for an answer, so I hang up. The amateurs of the steam radio listening to that particular late night show might notice a series of thumpings off-mike – it is, my dear reader, merely the ladies' chapter of the Edinburgh Keith Floyd appreciation society trying to break down my bedroom door!

THURSDAY 24 SEPTEMBER

A working breakfast with an urbane but slightly irrascible feature writer from the *Scotsman*, who at ten to eight presents me with a bottle of whisky whose label bears the legend, 'the inebriated newt'. Curiously, like my sandwich the night before, my breakfast of rashers, black and white pudding, kippers, potatoes et al is blindingly good.

I resist the temptation to pour the inebriated newt down his neck because I am dumbfounded by his first question which is, '*Should whisky be used in cooking like cognac is, in, for example, the recipe on page 73 of your book?*' Goddammit, the bloody man has actually read the book. I answer satisfactorily and tell him that in answer to the second part of his question, real Scots food is fine. I do not really think there is a case, however, for serving Aberdeen Angus beef with a whisky sauce. He adjusts his carefully knotted silk tie which bears the crest of some prestigious university, takes off his pince-nez and says, '*Hear, hear, dear boy, the only thing whisky is good for is drinking!*' We chat happily for about an hour, mainly about Colin Dean's decision to retire from rugby, and part the best of friends.

Outside, the magic wand has been waved again – the Ford has gone and in its place with an immaculate chauffeur in a deep-blue serge suit, polishing its radiator, stands a Mulliner Ward bodied Daimler. When the chauffeur sees us approach, he snaps to attention, slides me into the back, stows the luggage and starts up the mighty engine. I glance around the saloon and to my overwhelming joy about eighteen feet away across the chamois-leathered seats is a telephone.

I loosen my tie, stretch out among the cushions and start dialling the world as we purr along the road to Glasgow and a radio and television interview conducted in the BBC canteen where, with 87p's worth of ingredients from the 9 o'clock shop, they spring a little surprise on me which is simply to prepare a typical Scottish meal. Of course I rise to the occasion with aplomb, before doing the signing at 12.30 for the neat, well-dressed and enthusiastic citizens of Glasgow.

Escape from the signing intact and very happy. A brilliant lunch – working, of course (because I am being interviewed by the local paper) – of very fresh langoustines, lightly grilled, followed by a superb piece of turbot and a magnificent miniature steamed chocolate pudding served in, to my mind, one of the best restaurants in Scotland, Rogano.

From there, with barely time to quaff a quart of Muscat de Beaumes de Venise, on to the Jimmy Mack Show – one of the highlights of the tour. Jimmy has a bottle of Gevrais Chambertin for me and is one of the best radio show hosts in the business. Back in the Daimler and to the BBC for another signing in the bookshop where I am pounced upon by a BBC film crew who want to include me in a programme called 'See for Yourself', so I do my signing, perform brilliantly – naturally – leap into the back of the Daimler again for another little merry talk, followed by a signing in Edinburgh at 7 p.m. where I started from this morning with the bottle of inebriated newt.

To the delighted crowd in the bookshop I tell in essence the story of this book. And after a few cocktails in the bar of the Edinburgh Sheraton and a plate of appalling Chinese food in a nearby restaurant, the little boy has had a busy day and goes to bed.

FRIDAY 24 SEPTEMBER

Big winged bird from the airport to Heathrow. Little winged bird from Heathrow to Jersey. In a crowded bookshop full of happy people I lose count after 700 books. I can't take anymore and, by making a couple of telephone calls, manage to get out on the next flight for home.

'I THOUGHT A FAGGOT WAS A BUNCH OF STICKS TILL I DISCOVERED TELEVISION'

In which Floyd discovers that too many Faggots can get you into a Bugger's Muddle.

YOU LEARN SOME VERY FUNNY THINGS WHEN YOU'RE filming. Travelling around Great Britain making 'Floyd on Britain and Ireland' was quite an eye opener to me. You know how you never think your own home is very interesting until you have a foreign visitor staying with you, and out of politeness you take them round and then you discover all those interesting things? Same with us going to the Black Country. I mean I expected to find street after street of little red brick houses with pubs on the corners and ironmongers' shops and things: instead there was about 87 million square miles of Wimpey houses! There is no Black Country left. But we as television makers can't let little things like that interrupt what you're doing, so we went along to the Black Country Museum where they had recreated a corner of the Black Country, and this is where one cold – freezing – day, we stood gazing at the black, sludgy canal wondering what the hell we were going to do next. Now, read on . . .

TAPE OF FILMING AT THE BLACK COUNTRY MUSEUM

17 February 1988

KF – Keith Floyd
DP – David Pritchard
RJ – Richard James
MF – Mike Foren
RE – Richard Elliott

DP: It's very funny in television, you can actually do things and talk at the same time. OK? We'll start the whole thing on a two-shot and say, ever since we have been in the Black Country, which is what, you know, getting on for twenty minutes, it has been faggots and peas, faggots and peas, faggots and peas and every pub that we have been in has been full of faggots! – no, I mean, really, start it like that. I mean, these things are so important – so I said to the producer, you know, after the Christmas party – no, no, we can't use that! Let's get some faggots on this programme, so he said, 'So what's new!' OK, that's quite funny.

KF: Because of my eye-line problems, would it be OK if those people could either stand behind me or over there?

DP: Oh yeah, could you stand over there by that brown door because it just catches Keith's eye. Are we ready for a take? [*General discussion.*] Come on, let's go for it, otherwise we are going to lose the bloody whole thing.

MF: OK, speed.

DP: Action.

KF: You don't have to be in the Black Country for very long before you realize that the faggot plays a very significant role in the culture here. I mean they have them on the walls in the pubs, they have them in museums, etc., etc. – Richard knows all about faggots, don't you?

RJ: Oh yes, I am the well-known Faggot King of the Black Country, Keith. I have been making them for many years in the Black Country, and the recipe that I have got has been handed down from generation to generation and all I am doing . . .'

KF: They all say that [*laughs*], I think we should start again.

DP: We'll stop there. I liked that, it's wonderful.

KF: Excellent, it's only me that's not very good.

DP: Turn over please. OK, off we go.

KF: [*Repeats intro again . . .*]

RJ: I have been making faggots here in the Black Country for close on fifteen years, from my professional days in the hotels to keep the traditional Black Country faggots going.

KF: But it's a long road for you to have left from the smart kitchens of the Hilton. Is there a future in Black Country cooking?'

RJ: Years ago in this area we had all the heavy industry, now that has all gone it's tourism and the food is a part of this.

KF: Well, let's have a look at some.

DP: Shall we just stop there a minute? Let's have a conversation, it just seems like a brochure for the Black Country tourist guide, it sounded like a prepared statement. I would prefer a looser conversation. Is that OK? OK, turn over – it's better to say these things now than wait until we are editing the sequence in the studios.

MF: OK, speed.

DP: Off you go.

KF: This place is full of faggots, and with me, oh Christ, that sounds like Alan Whicker! [*laughs*].

DP: OK, and again, on a single shot this time, Richard. OK off you go.

KF: [*Reels off Black Country speech again, Richard James mentions the words Black Country at least four times.*] Let's look at these faggots. I am not at all happy about what I am doing.

DP: Right, cut.

KF: Can we go for a walk in the garden?

DP: OK, let's go for a walk in the indoor garden. What's it look like? [*to Mike Foren. Explains to RJ that it does not matter if it all goes wrong.*] So let's just go for it. Let's ditch the pub bit. OK, turn over.

MF: OK, speed.

DP: Off you go.

KF: [*Repeats intro again – no good, KF not happy.*]

DP: Nearly right, it sounds good. OK, and action.

KF: I have been coming to the Black Country for at least three hours . . . What we are going to try and do now, Mike? [*wrong name*].

DP: Don't worry, we can get this by Tuesday! Right, OK.

KF: OK, I know how to do it now.

DP: OK, turn over.

MF: Speed.

DP: Off you go.

KF: To misquote Spike Milligan, why isn't there a monument to faggots in this land? If it's good enough to eat, then it's good enough to stand. They are so important here. There should be national recognition. Now Richard, you've got thirty seconds to explain all about Black Country cooking without mentioning the word Black Country once.

RJ: Well, here in the area . . .

KF: What's the area, Richard?

RJ: The Black Country . . .

KF: That's one.

RJ: We are proud of the traditional food.

KF: [*Shows faggots to camera.*] I'm going to taste them if I may, Ow! [*Burns fingers.*]

DP: Keep going.

KF: They love it when I do things like that. I had a late night last night, that's the truth of it. I will just have a new plate, a new drop of gravy and I will start this all over again with my faggot juice and my faggot and a few mushy peas. This is hopeless, it's really hopeless, I don't know what to do next.

DP: Cut. OK, we'll put the faggots back — we're nearly there. That was brilliant, it's not easy. Have a quick swig of your medicine, Keith.

[*Mike Foren suggests doing a few cut-aways, as the take was so good, and picking up from the point where Keith picks up a new plate. David agrees.*]

DP: OK, we'll start with a close up of the hands holding the plate and a spoon. Keep in close up, Richard.

KF: Where will I start now?

RE: Pick the plate up and come up into frame.

MF: If we start from picking up the plate, put the gravy on and then put the faggot on after the gravy, we'll find a point to pick it up.

DP: Yeah, that'll work, right, can I just explain; clean plate, whack a little bit of gravy on and you may have noticed the edit point there, and then those delicious faggots, and then say, now why did you leave a brilliant job in the Hilton for the humble faggot? Taste it and what I would like you to also say is that they are not those frozen meatballs, they are real faggots with real cawl and hearts, is that OK? [*to Keith*].

KF: Yes, great.

DP: OK, pick the plate up and turn over.

MF: OK, speed.

DP: And off you go, Keith.

KF: So with my new plate I will put my faggot juice on, this is in quite the wrong order, of course, then one of these wonderful faggots. I mean, this is very odd Richard, I don't actually understand why you gave up the life of glamour in London. Do you think that these faggots are appreciated, Richard?

RJ: I hope so, these are very popular in the area of the Black Country.

KF: That's two.

RJ: They are made from fresh offal . . .

KF: This is a masterpiece. Anyway, the point about this programme actually is it's called 'Floyd', so I am going to tell you how to make faggots.

RJ: Shall I take your coat, Keith?

KF: OK, Richard (E) a quick spin around the ingredients. The essentials are pig's liver, pig's lights, heart, cawl, onions, sage and breadcrumbs. [*Singing as he minces the offal*] With a spong in my heart. What could be better than to be greeted when you get home by a couple of warm faggots? I am now going on a magical mystery tour.

DP: OK, cut, very good, excellent [*claps*], can I look at it back?

MF: There is a problem with Richard standing there, he was still in shot, he needs to go around the corner.

DP: I'm sorry, it was smashing, Richard, otherwise. That was a lovely take, a brilliant take – Keith, can I have a word? [*Goes through with Keith how to introduce ingredients, which ones to point out.*] I'm very pleased with that you know, I like that 'with a spong in my heart' bit. OK, turn over please.

MF: OK, speed.

DP: Stand by and action.

KF: [*Starts again with a new plate and puts on the faggots and mushy peas, calls Richard James Mike again.*] I'm sorry to keep calling you Mike, but you so look like that guy Mike Harding.

[*Richard Elliott interrupts and apologizes for having jolted the camera.*]

DP: Cut. Stand nearer to Keith, Richard (J), you are too far away. OK.

MF: OK, speed.

DP: Off you go.

KF: [*Starts again . . .*] Why did you give up London?

RJ: Well there's nothing wrong with that, coming back to your roots.

[*KF then starts to cook faggots.*]

KF: In Somerset where I come from we make them differently, but first of all we'll spin around the ingredients . . . in Somerset we poach the pluck in water with sage and onion [*KF dries*].

DP: OK, cut it there. I was wondering if that child screaming was a problem. Was it OK? [*to Richard, the sound man*]. Yes. Shall we go again, do you mind?

KF: No of course not, I'm just sorry that I'm not doing it very well.

DP: We're nearly there.

KF: Oh dear, oh dear.

DP: What we're getting is good, there's lots of information, don't be put off and don't worry. And Richard, the less you sound like the tourist guide, the better.

RJ: Well, I've cut that out.

DP: Yeah, chuck it all out, we're not interested in that, we're interested in the food, the heritage and the pride of this particular region. Happy?

MF: Can we take some cutaways because that take was so good?

[*Richard E takes some shots.*]

MF: OK, thank you, Richard.

DP: Right, I'm happy.

MF: Recording.

DP: We will be done by 12.30. OK, let's go for it once more. Turn over.

MF: Speed.

DP: Action.

KF: [*Starts again with the plate and starts to make faggots.*]

DP: Cut, I think we can go again, it needs more zest – it's nobody's fault, it just needs more zest. OK, turn over. Get Frances outside to give those guys some money [*meaning JCB operators*]. Turn over, let's go for it.

MF: Speed.

DP: Can we tell those people in the restaurant to shut up? Turn over please – this is brilliant fun, isn't it?

MF: Speed.

DP: And action.

KF: [*Goes again*] We now have about eleven plates of half-eaten faggots in the sink as I haven't been very successful today . . .

[*Rest of take goes brilliantly.*]

DP: OK, cut – happy? Happy Mike? That was good, wasn't it?

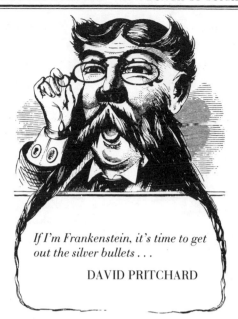

If I'm Frankenstein, it's time to get out the silver bullets . . .

DAVID PRITCHARD

EPILOGUE

THE EVENING BREEZE STIRS THE COCONUT PALMS, AND THEY flail and shimmer like the silver rotors of some heavenly gyrocopter as the sun slips quickly into the sea, and releases the soft black night that seeps across the sky like spilt ink. Across the island to the ocean yellow lights of cabins, bungalows, tin-roofed stores, bars, gas stations and churches splutter on. They are not as bright as the evening star.

The wind drops and for a long eerie moment there is silence as the world holds its breath. Here comes the night. Bats and huge black moths stall-dive into the mosquito screens, hungry for the light that seeps through the window. The evening orchestra of frogs tune-up for the symphony. At six-thirty the band begins to play. If I stretched out my hand I could touch the moon, a big mother-of-pearl button, shining behind the banana groves. But I'm too lazy to move from this reclining seat. A big lizard runs along the edge of the swimming pool, sees me and turns himself to stone daring me to stare him out. A sun-tanned woman steps serenely into the dark blue water of the pool and glides across, barely causing a ripple. I lift the top off a Carib. The pale, weak beer tastes very good. It is cold and frothy. A cruise ship, its lights blazing, is creeping across the night. It looks obscene. I sip my beer and watch it disappear round the headland. The woman climbs out of the pool and shakes the water from her body on to my hot skin. 1 know how the wounded beggar felt when the Samaritan crossed the road and bathed his wounds in olive oil. It is 1 January, 1988.

'Now hold on a minute, Floyd,' I hear you say. 'Have we changed books, or what? Have you lost your marbles? Are you dreaming, or did you want to send this to Mills and Boon?'

Dear reader, I shall choose to ignore your questions – it is 7.15 p.m. and we are going to bathe, change and drift down the path – lit by flickering lamps where frogs are stationed waiting for insects drawn to the light (they sit in the same place each night), for dinner. Tonight it is lemon soup, grilled red snapper with ginger, carrots and sweet cucumbers. Dessert is rum and raisin ice-cream. There are only half a dozen couples

staying at the plantation and, despite the entreaties of our 'hosts' to treat
the place like a country house hotel, we manage to sip our planters
punches – with freshly grated nutmeg – in the corner alone. Alongside,
ageing Americans pore over plans of bungalows they are planning to
build, or hope to, if the dollar recovers.

At 8.20 p.m. dinner is served with shy reverence by serene
islanders on the terrace. It is very warm and the moon, now high, beams
over the Caribbean.

'Shine on, silvery moon, please, shine a lot of light on me.'

Two million years ago we left the scudding clouds and squalls of England,
to sit on the side of this extinct volcano. The flight from Heathrow was fun
– BA upgraded us and we travelled in great style. We landed in mid-
afternoon and stepped into a furnace. Like smothering your face in a hot
towel that Indian restaurants give you. Only this towel had been soaked in
salt and aviation fuel.

It's good to wake up and see the ocean and watch the cloud that
sits, like a halo, over the summit. It's too steep to climb easily and enter
the rain forest. I'm just happy to know it's there. While we eat our
breakfast little black birds with red breasts peck at the sugar on our table.
The fruit juice is canned, but the paw-paw is fresh. The fried free-range
eggs, and crispy bacon from the fat black pigs, is divine.

The gardeners greet us with a shy smile and upturned palms.
Gentle body language that embarrasses me, perhaps a legacy of former
cruel times when their ancestors were bred on stud farms, like the one at
Gingerland just over the hill.

After breakfast we take the Mini-Moke, painted bright red and
lovingly polished like a fire engine, and go down to Charlestown looking
for soul food. Past the red, corrugated-roof church where Nelson was
married – the register, decaying fast, is still there to see; past government
house and its sleepy sentries; past the Old Bath Hotel, glorious in the
eighteenth century but now just another rotting monument to white
colonial rule. We go bouncing down Main Street with untidy stores piled
high with bright cotton dresses, tins of evaporated milk, primus stoves
and galvanized buckets, past a dozen churches and a bar, avoiding a
chicken clucking across the potted road. The locals drive four-wheel-drive
Japanese pick-up trucks, using the derelict Morris Oxfords and Cambrid-
ges to keep chickens in. On the jetty they're lifting a new Mazda from the

open hold of a sailing boat. I'd like to paint the piles of timber, the carton of loo rolls, the crates of beer, the bags of chickens and the steel girders that are stacked haphazardly around. Paint the big US coast-guard cutter that, bristling with antennae and cannons, looks so modern, so out of place here. The stalls in the market are concrete slabs; there's not much for sale, but I like the chillies and bananas, red and yellow. Unella's Restaurant is a drab concrete balcony on the waterfront. The meat curry with paw-paw chutney is brilliant.

It's too hot to work in the afternoon so we sunbathe and swim, make love and watch the sun slide down to the sea. You can hear a gardener slashing rhythmically at a large hedgerow with a machete, in time with the music pouring from his ghetto blaster:

'Under the boardwalk, down by the sea, on a blanket with my baby is where I'll be . . .'

I'm sitting here under the volcano in ninety degrees of Caribbean sunshine trying to review. To focus on the events of the last few months is like looking at the Rockies though the wrong end of a telescope – the mountains look like molehills.

I mean what is divorce anyway? On the bottom line it is only money. Thank God the franchise affair never got off the ground – instead of sipping beers and writing a book I'd be worried to death about the lousy food they'd be serving under the name of Floyd. So what if some people want to sue you for a percentage of your income for life, it's only money. They'd never understand that:

> You climbed on to my carousel
> I didn't ask you for the fare
> And now it's stopped turning
> You say I don't care

So why bother to explain? If they have to ask, they'll never know.

Do you know something else? If Pritchard parachuted on to this island right now, I'd be quite happy to take him down to the white sands of the Nisbet Plantation and buy him a charcoal-grilled fresh crayfish for lunch and watch the pelicans play with the wind. For an hour or two.

Zetland Plantation
Nevis, West Indies, January 1988.

As Camus said (and he was another outsider):

>   Do not walk in front of me, I will not follow;
>   Do not walk behind me, I will not lead;
>   Walk beside me and be my friend.